Marry Me

Giving Jesus My Yes

Kay Neal

ISBN: 978-0-578-37379-9

Editor: Mary Ruth Erb

Cover Design: Mary Ruth Erb

This book is dedicated to my children, my grandchildren, and all of the generations to come. May you come to know the God who adores you and calls you His beloved bride. This book is the tale of my great love story and the legacy I leave for you.

Acknowledgments

Above all I want to thank the Holy Spirit for helping me put on paper the things I have longed to share about God's goodness and His love. This book has come out of my life experience and my intimate relationship with Him. Without the Holy Spirit as my teacher, I would have absolutely nothing to share.

My precious husband—thank you for championing me, believing in me, and investing in this project. Your support has meant the world to me, and I'm forever grateful to have you by my side. I love you always and forever.

My children—all of you have taught me things and grown me as a mother. Thank you for giving me second chances. Thank you for forgiving me. Thank you for being one of the greatest blessings of my life and making me a mother. I love you all to the moon and back.

My parents—your shared passion for the Word of God is an inspiration and a legacy I am grateful to inherit. Thank you for continually covering me and my family in prayer. I love you both immensely!

My circle of friends (you know who you are)—I would not have finished this book if not for your constant encouragement and prayers. Thank you for lifting me up, speaking into my life, and being a safe place to share my heart. You are all gems!

My Instagram family—thank you for taking an interest in my life and valuing what I have to say. So many of you have lifted me up and encouraged me in this process. Thank you for your support!

My editor—I could not have done this without you! Thank you for pulling out the gold in me and believing in this message.

Contents

Everyone's Looking for Their Great Love Story

Everyone is looking for that love of a lifetime—a divine romance that fills their heart with joy and ignites them with passion. The truth is, we were all born with an innate desire for romance. God actually designed us that way.

Look at today's best selling books, movies, and TV shows. Hollywood has capitalized on the fact that everyone is desperately looking for "their person." We've come to believe that if we just find our great love story, everything in our lives will be different, and we will finally have the one thing we have been missing all along: someone who will not only love us unconditionally, but also never leave or break our heart. We have bought into the lie that finding the love of our lives will make us complete, and the wounds in our soul will somehow magically disappear.

But even the best earthly relationships fall short and cannot totally fulfill us—because they were never designed to. When I married my husband, we were so in love we felt like we couldn't live without each other. My husband showed me more unconditional love than anyone I had ever known. And yet, as wonderful as this was, even his love for me couldn't heal the deep places in my heart that only God Himself could reach.

When I radically encountered the manifest presence of Jesus and surrendered to Him, I found the healing love I had been searching for all of my life. The answer had always been union—marriage—with Jesus.

I believe Jesus has been inviting us into union with Him all along. When He took His last breath on the cross, He cried out the Hebrew word *kalah*. This word has two meanings. The one we all know is "It is finished." The other meaning is "bride." Perhaps what Jesus was really saying was, "It is finished, my bride."[1] Can you hear Him asking, "Will you marry me?"

Chapter 1

Where It all Started

I remember being as young as three years old and feeling inferior to the other little girls in my preschool. One winter I begged my mom to let me wear this fancy, yellow, organdy dress to preschool every single day for a whole week. I suppose this dress made me feel a wee bit better about myself, maybe even pretty. Later on, when I got a little older, my mom told me: "Kay, it didn't matter if the girls at your preschool were as ugly as a mud fence, if they had pretty, long hair, you would think they were beautiful."

There I was, only three or four years old, and the enemy was already beginning to sow seeds of self-hatred and inferiority into my young heart. Little did anyone realize, those seeds would one day grow into a massive tree.

Standard of Beauty

I grew up watching every beauty pageant that came on television. Watching beauty pageants was a main event in my home. I would watch them with my mom and dad, as well as my good friend Waynette Stinson when I was at my grandmother's house. Outward beauty was something of great value in my home growing up, and I was painfully aware, even at a very young age, that I was falling very short in this department.

At the tender age of nine, I unwittingly came across some Playboy magazines. When I saw the pictures of airbrushed models with perfect figures, I thought this must be the kind of woman all men really wanted. I started to believe I needed to look as close to this as possible. My belief went so deep that I actually thought when a man got married, he married what he thought was the best he could get, but deep down, he still wanted that perfect, airbrushed woman. This impression was embedded into my heart and became a moment of impact that shaped my life.

A Mix of Emotions

By the time I was in the sixth grade, I was already starting to feel fat and ugly, even though I was one of the most popular girls in my class that year. I was never really what you would have called overweight, but I was certainly more developed than the other girls my age. This really bothered me, and I wanted to change the way I looked. I decided to go on a diet, and I continued to try different ones all throughout the sixth grade.

The next year I started the seventh grade at Woodlawn, a large junior high that was also a High school. I was a small fish in a very large pond. The only people I knew there were the few kids from my elementary school who had come along with me. I was basically starting all over again. I already had deep-rooted insecurities, so this was not an easy year for me.

When school ended that year, I headed to my maternal grandmother's house where I spent most of my summer every year. That particular summer had a huge impact on my already damaged self-image. I had braces, my face was now covered with acne, and to make things worse, I decided to put sun-in on my hair, which turned it a horrid shade of orange. My hormones were very out of whack, so I also put on at least ten pounds during those few short months.

Changing Schools

Before I started eighth grade, I begged my parents to put me in a private, college-preparatory school. I had convinced myself that if I could get a really good education and then go onto vet school, I would gain the approval and acceptance of my dad's side of the family, who I had visited that summer.

When I started eighth grade at Episcopal High, I felt like a total misfit. My dad dropped me off at school in his work truck, while the other parents pulled up in their Cadillacs, Lincoln Town Cars, and Jaguars. To make things worse, almost all of the kids who attended this school had been together since pre-school, and I was an outsider.

In spite of the fact that I was learning a lot, studying very hard, and making good grades, I still felt the sting of rejection on every front. Every day our school cafeteria served these amazing, hot rolls, and you could go back as many times as you wanted. I always went back for seconds. Then when I got home from school, the first thing I did was head for the fridge. I began eating more and more, subconsciously trying to bury my feelings of rejection. In spite of my overeating, I was still not that big, but I was definitely bigger than the other girls my age who still had not gone through puberty.

New Highs and New Lows

While I was at Episcopal, my mom gave me a book to read that would ultimately start drawing my heart toward God. The name of the book was, *18, No Time to Waste*.[1] The story was about a girl who was a very popular cheerleader. When she gave her life to Jesus, she impacted her whole high school before being tragically killed in a car accident. Reading about her life made me see something I wanted in mine, even though I didn't really understand what it was. Around the same time I read the book, I was showing horses with a girl who seemed to really stand out. Later on, I found out she was a strong Christian. Jesus was beginning to reveal Himself to me by putting people in my path who loved Him.

Unfortunately, there were also some people in my path who made life harder that year. Because I was thicker than the other girls, some of the boys in my class started referring to me as *roast* as a word play on my last name *Coast*. I got really sick of being the chubby girl at school and feeling the rejection that went along with it. I began to starve myself to lose weight. All of my dieting attempts had failed miserably, so starving seemed like my only option. Every day after school was out, I headed to the barn to ride and train my horse for show season. I starved myself for two weeks, drinking only a couple of cups of coffee and eating one ice cream bar for the whole day. I dropped ten to twelve pounds in only two or three weeks.

Right after this, my mom took me shopping for new clothes, and it was a really special event for me. I felt so much love and approval from her, and it was wonderful. I felt good about myself, for the first time in a very long time.

Popular at Last

The next school year I wanted to go back to Woodlawn (the high school I had left in the seventh grade). When I returned for my freshman year, I went from being the ugly, chubby girl, to being considered the pretty girl with the good figure. I felt totally rejected in the eight grade, and now here I was in ninth grade, one of the most popular girls at school overnight.

This sealed the deal and a core decision was made. I had to stay thin, whatever the cost might be. Dieting and starving became a way of life. I would eat normal one day and then starve the next. After a while, this got old, and that's when I remembered Ipecac syrup. I stumbled upon it by accident in the seventh grade, and I used it once to make myself throw up when I had eaten too much. That moment planted a seed in my mind, and when I couldn't handle the diets and starvation anymore, I thought, *What if I just throw my food up when I overeat, or eat something I feel guilty for?*

When I first started throwing up, I would purposely forget to feed my horse so I had a reason to go out to the barn when supper was over. I would head out there where I could not be heard and gag myself until I thought every ounce of food I had eaten was out of my stomach. At first it was just my dinner, but later it would become everything I ate. I would eat, throw up, and then be starving again. So then I would eat again and gorge myself because I was so hungry. Then I would be miserable, so I would throw it up again. I became very weak because not only did I throw up my food, but I also started throwing up any liquid for the fear of feeling bloated. This constant cycle of binging and purging would end up taking over everything in my life.

When Christmas came around that year, I went to a special church service with my boyfriend. In the midst of all the brokenness in my life, God was still drawing me, and I felt His presence during the service. Unfortunately, not long after this event, my mom caught me throwing up. Even though I was totally humiliated, and I tried to stop, I just couldn't.

Nowhere to Turn but God

As far back as I can remember, my family only went to church on Christmas and Easter. I remember my mom praying with me as a little girl before bed, but other than that, I knew very little about God. Right before my eating disorder began, my mom started going to church on a regular basis. She suggested I come with her and go down to the senior high class that her best friend taught. That Sunday her friend talked about the Holy Spirit. Then she said something that took me completely off guard. She said, "My best friend has the Holy Spirit and speaks in tongues." I knew her best friend was my mom, and she must be talking about her. That night I asked my mom if I could hear her pray in tongues. When I was going to bed, she came into my room and prayed for me. I felt the presence of God all over the room, and I was in awe. I told my mom, "Whatever this is, I want it."

The next day, my mom gave me a book to read by Catherine Marshall called *Something More*.[2] She told me to read the chapter in it about the Holy Spirit. Not long after, she took me over to a couples home she had met through friends so they could pray for me to receive the Holy Spirit. I did not speak in tongues that night, but I knew I was definitely born again. When I woke up the next day, the sky seemed bluer and the birds were singing a new song. I felt truly alive for the first time, and everything inside of me felt different. A few weeks before this, my mom had given me a Bible, and I had tried to read it, but it was like reading Latin. When I picked up my Bible the morning after we prayed, I could not put it down. My eyes were truly open, and everything I read in my Bible made perfect sense. I knew I was reading God's love letter to me. Here I was, this messed up kid in the beginning of a horrible eating disorder, but I knew He loved me. This was all I had ever wanted—unconditional love.

Even though I was born again, I still continued to struggle with my eating disorder. In spite of my failure, I loved Jesus, and I knew He loved me. I started attending a house church on Wednesday nights, and I was able to make friends with some older young adults who became like brothers and sisters. During this time, my dad also gave his life to Jesus and was born again. We started attending a Charismatic Episcopalian church as a family, and even though it was very different from anything I had experienced, I really loved it. Honestly, I was just grateful to be born again and completely overwhelmed that I could know God on a personal level.

Getting Help

Not long after this, some Christian friends told my parents about a counseling center in Abilene, Texas, where I could get help with my eating disorder. We ended up going out there at the very beginning of my sophomore year. No one really knew how to properly deal with eating disorders back then. They tried to address the breakdown between my parents and I first. From what I remember, they focused a lot of their attention on my parents' mistakes during counseling. Since I had always been the problem, I felt a huge sense of relief. For the first time, I felt like I was really being seen and heard.

Before we went to Abilene, my dad caught me with my cigarettes in my socks and took them away. I had started smoking in the ninth grade to try and keep myself from eating. While we were in counseling, they told my parents to let me smoke because they thought it might help me to stop binging. This just shows how little the professionals knew about why people develop eating disorders, or the real roots of this destructive behavior.

When we came home from Abilene, my parents laid down a list of rules for me to follow, and they set some boundaries hoping that it would help us both. My dad then gave me a beautiful, green Volkswagen Karmann Ghia he had restored for me. They gave me an allowance and a budget. The hope was that I would start to take responsibility for my life. I would have plenty of freedom, if I chose well.

Not long after this, I wrecked my beautiful, little Volkswagen. While I was driving to school one morning, I leaned over to light a cigarette and plowed into a mailbox. That was it. I already felt like a total failure, and this just confirmed it. The failure and the shame felt so overwhelming that I couldn't face my parents. After school, I drove my battered, but drivable little car to the bus station and bought a one-way ticket to Abilene. I knew there were people there who would show me unconditional love in spite of myself. When I got there, I called this lady I had counseled with, hoping she would take me in. Before she could do this, I had to go through a certain protocol. I was first sent to the local girls' home for about two weeks, but then I moved in with an amazing woman named Bernice, who I met from the counseling center.

Even though Bernice was a strong Christian, and I loved everything about her, she and I were from two different church backgrounds, and I missed my old church and friends. I began to feel more and more disconnected from the Lord during this time, despite still reading my Bible and talking to God. The guilt I was carrying over my eating disorder ate me up inside, and my heart became less and less tender toward God because of the shame I felt. As a result, my eating disorder just got worse and worse. I ate to numb my pain, and I purged to control my weight.

Many nights I would get up in the middle of the night to cook and eat for hours, then throw up several times so I could start again. There were times Bernice knew what I was doing because she would hear me in her kitchen. In spite of this insanity, she overlooked my outward behavior and saw my heart. I never once remember her fussing at me, even when I felt I totally deserved it. She was kind and loving and a picture of God's perfect love, but still, it wasn't enough to make me whole.

While I was still in Texas, the counseling center sent me to the hospital. The nurse made me get on the scales, and I weighed only eighty-five pounds at five-foot-five. I would stay way below a normal body weight for a very long time. Some days I was so weak that I would ask to go to the bathroom during class. I would then curl up on the floor of a stall and fall asleep until the next bell rang.

While I was living with Bernice, I continued to go to counseling at the same center I had gone to with my parents. It was great most of the time, and I loved the people there, but sometimes their methods felt very off. There was one session in particular that made me feel really uncomfortable, and it changed how I felt about getting counseling there. Shortly after this happened, my grandfather died, and my mom drove to Abilene to bring me back for his funeral. Once I was back in Louisiana, I realized how much I missed my friends, and I wanted to go back to my old school. After this, I stayed in Louisiana and never went back to the counseling center in Abilene.

Home Again

When I came home, I went back to school and got my car back, which my dad had fixed for me while I was gone. I also ended up getting back with all of the friends I had before I became a Christian. Now those same friends had become involved in things I had never done before, and they were definitely not a great influence on me. I became even more rebellious, and I started to drift away from God.

After tenth grade ended, my parents had had enough of my rebellion and eating disorder, and they threatened to kick me out. They said I had to go to a ministry where they did prayer counseling if I wanted to continue living at home. I was only sixteen, and I had no way to support myself. I knew I had no choice but to do what they asked. I agreed to go, but at this point, my heart was stone cold toward God.

Back On Track with God

Right before we left to go to prayer counseling in Florida, my mom and dad sent me to church to pick up some young ministry students who were going to stay with us for a few days. When I got to the church, I had to go inside to find them so they could ride home with me. When I went inside, there was a room full of young students worshiping God and singing. As soon as I entered that room, the love of God broke through my rebellious heart, and I melted in His presence. I came home that night with a totally changed heart, and I was ready to go to prayer counseling.

The prayer counseling center was in Destin, Florida, at a Spirit-filled Episcopalian church. They walked me through many prayers of repentance and deliverance, and before I knew it, my life was back on track again. My eating disorder did not completely go away, but I did get much better.

After that summer, I had more of a normal school year. I started working and dating, and I went to several proms at different schools. One prom I will never forget was at Catholic High. A local band was playing that night and one of the band members had grown up next door to me. After seeing me that night, he called and asked me to go out with him. I was only seventeen, and he was twenty-two. I told him no, but said if he wanted to come to church with me he could. He took me up on my offer. The first night I brought him he cried like a baby through the whole message, and afterwards He wanted to receive Jesus. I was not expecting this at all, but it was pretty incredible.

Seventeen and Engaged to Be Married

As crazy as this sounds, a couple of months later, we got engaged. Thankfully, we did not end up getting married, and at the end of my junior year, we broke up. My parents actually loved the guy, but they knew this would not be the best thing for me. Fortunately, they played it cool and never put up a big fuss about things, hoping it would run its course. They told me later they were afraid that if they said anything to stop me from getting married, I might run off and elope just to spite them. That summer we went our separate ways, and it ended as fast as it started.

When I entered my senior year the next fall, I was finally at a normal weight. I had started keeping food down more and more, in an attempt to get over my eating disorder before I got married. I still binged and purged sometimes, but it was nothing like it had been at one time. My senior year was pretty uneventful. I was serving God, going to school, and trying to figure out what my next step was.

Shortly after I graduated from high school, we had a guest speaker come to my church. Right before the service, I tried to make a deal with God. I told Him I wanted to go off to college and have a good time for the first two years, and then I would do what He wanted me to do. At church that night, I came under such a strong conviction of the Holy Spirit that I cried through the whole service. While this was happening, I clearly heard God ask me, "Do you want to waste two years of your life?" I told Him no, and I surrendered everything I knew to surrender at that moment.

Finding My Way

After graduating from high school, my dad and I took a portage canoe trip to Canada. We planned every detail together, and it meant the world to do something so special with him. While we were on our way from Louisiana to Canada, we stopped to check out several colleges I was interested in. The one I really wanted to go to was in Montana. Being that I had always been a horse girl, my dream was to go to college there, marry a Christian cowboy, and raise horses. My parents were not keen on sending me this far away since I was just getting my life back on track, and my eating disorder was under control. Being that far from home didn't seem like a great idea. Although I was very disappointed, I understood.

Shortly after this trip, I moved into my own place and got a job at a large pediatric clinic. I loved my job, and working there inspired me to pursue pediatric nursing. I applied to LSU and decided I wanted to be a nurse at St. Judes Children's Hospital. Working with sick children was what I knew I wanted to do, and I believed God was calling me to St. Judes.

Someone Who Loved Me Without Condition

While I was still working at the Pediatric clinic, I met my husband. Not long after we had been together, I knew I needed to tell him about all I had walked through and where I was now in terms of my eating disorder. When I shared my story, he showed me nothing but compassion. God had given him His heart for me, and he loved me unconditionally.

After we got married, I still had my good days and bad days. When I would have a really bad day, my husband loved me without condemnation or judgment. He would always remind me that my eating disorder was not who I was, and it did not define me. He never lost sight of who God had called me to be, or even the woman he believed I was. Over time, I got better and better, but I still had my slip ups every now and again. They usually did not last long, and they got further and further apart as time went on. I always felt free to tell my husband when I was struggling, even though I was still very ashamed. He never got upset with me, but he *was* concerned about the effects it was having on my health. In spite of it all, he never doubted that one day I would be completely free.

Many times I thought about reaching out for professional help, but I had no idea where to turn in those days. There was so little understanding of eating disorders at that time. The other reason I did not pursue professional help was because of finances. We were a young family, and with my husband right out of college, finances were a big concern.

Dreams of Children

When I got married, I was worried I wouldn't be able to have children because of all the damage I had done to my body. We started trying almost right away, and I was able to have five healthy children in just seven short years. With each child I was still struggling with my eating disorder on some level, but I gained a normal amount of weight with each pregnancy. After each baby was born, I was able to breastfeed, and with this I also carried some extra baby weight. My husband loved me just the way I was, and he told me he would be fine if I never lost the extra weight. These words were like the balm of Gilead to my heart. I felt so loved and accepted by him.

With my last pregnancy, I finally felt like I had the tools I needed to walk free. In the past, anything that was not diet food or healthy was considered bad food in my eyes. If I ate anything fattening, I always felt guilty, so I just ate more, and then I felt like I needed to throw it up. Everything changed when I learned that there was no bad food if I only ate when I was hungry. This was very freeing. I could eat anything I wanted if I ate for hunger, stopped when I was full, and didn't eat until I was hungry again. I learned to pay attention to hunger, but no food was off limits this way.

Even when I started eating for hunger, it was still very hard because I was not used to feeling full. I had never allowed myself to feel overly full without throwing it up. I was also concerned I would gain a ton of weight if I ever totally stopped. Having an eating disorder had absolutely destroyed my metabolism, so I gained weight very easily.

When I got pregnant with my last baby, I knew if I gained a little extra weight, people would just assume it was because I was pregnant. If I did get heavy, they would have no idea it was because I was no longer purging every time I overate. I had really bad morning sickness, but in my third month of pregnancy, I completely stopped throwing up. Many times it felt like I was sweating blood because I wanted to throw up so badly. I struggled desperately, but I never gave in. I knew if I gave in once, I would go into a downhill spiral, and I was not sure how long it would take to get myself back on track. Throughout my last pregnancy, and for several years after I had my last child, I walked in total freedom. I never threw up even once, but in my heart, I still felt like I was just one slip away from going back into bondage.

One Step Forward, Two Steps Back

I had no slip ups at all until after I went through a really hard season in my marriage. My husband and I made it to the other side of this trial, but I got very thin during that time. I lost weight simply because I was too stressed to eat, and I stayed very thin for a long time. Eventually, I started to gain some of the weight I had lost, and I struggled again for a short time. I had bought all new clothes when I was thin, and I put a lot of pressure on myself to keep wearing them.

During my setback, I called my good friend and told her I was struggling. She prayed for me and told me to do a three day water fast. I did this, and once again, I got my footing. After that very short setback, I went for five long years without even one slip. Then, I started struggling again. I was walking through a heartbreaking situation that was completely out of my control. A woman in my life was making terrible choices that were affecting not only me, but also two of my daughters. This situation triggered me to binge and purge. Once I started up again, I would be okay for long periods, and then I would be struggling again. I slipped in and out of this cycle for years. Most of the time I could maintain my victory through my discipline of eating only for hunger, but inside I never felt totally free. I was starting to see the pattern of wanting to binge and purge when life felt out of my control.

Finally Free

Even with all the years of struggling, I never lost hope that one day I would be totally and completely free. Many times in my past, I had amazing encounters with the Lord, but they never brought me into permanent freedom from my eating disorder. I talk more about this in the next chapter, but after Hurricane Katrina hit Louisiana, my world started falling apart. During this time, I came to the end of myself in a way I had never experienced before. After a radical encounter with the love of God (which I also explain in subsequent chapters) I fully yielded every room in my heart to Him. Over the next year, my life began to completely transform as I let His love take me over and heal the broken places in my heart. One day, several months into this journey, I was reading my Bible when a verse jumped off the page and went straight into my heart.

For by the one offering He has perfected forever and completely cleansed those who are being sanctified [bringing each believer to spiritual completion and maturity] (Hebrews 10:14 AMP).

Jesus had already made me perfect by His one sacrifice. I took these words of spirit and life into my being, and they totally changed how I saw myself. I had read this verse many times before, but on this particular day, I actually heard it in my spirit. It went through every fiber of my being, and I saw it with true revelation for the first time. All these years, I had been trying to make myself perfect. I thought if I could just be obedient, it would make me clean, but the truth was, I was already clean.

> *The words I have spoken over you have already cleansed you. So you must remain in life-union with me, for I remain in life-union with you (John 15:3–4 TPT).*

I stopped focusing on the struggle to walk in freedom, and I just stayed in union. I looked at Jesus, and I was perfect in His eyes. I believed it, and it became my reality. The veil of religion that blinded me was removed, and what He said about me in His Word became my identity rather than my eating disorder. I was already perfected. I did not need to try and perfect myself! After this, I never looked back. Even in the hardest of seasons, I never binged and purged again.

In the past, I had been through many types of counseling and even deliverance ministry, but as this one truth took root that day, it brought the anchor my soul needed to walk into total and complete freedom. This time I knew it would be different. The truth became such a part of me that there was no temptation to ever return. I knew in my heart of heart's that I was perfected and completely cleansed, and I walked in this from that point on.

The Root

Months into my freedom, the Holy Spirit revealed that I had been dealing with a triple stronghold of fear, shame and control, which had now been completely dismantled by one word from God. My fear was being rejected, my shame had been my binging, and my control was purging. When life felt like it was falling apart, and I could not control things, binging and purging had been the way I dealt with my pain. In all of the counseling I had done, the root of my problem was never brought to the surface. The focus had always been on my binging. I was told I had a problem with food. Once I stopped purging, I never binged ever again. Food had never been the problem.

After so many years of trying and failing, I had almost given up hope that I could be completely free. It honestly felt like a dream. I had found true freedom through union with Jesus, and all I wanted was more of Him. Overcoming my eating disorder was such a huge moment for me, but still, God had much more in store. My journey had really *just begun*.

Chapter 2

How I Came to the End of Myself

In 2004 I was introduced to a product that changed my life, and I believed it could change other people's as well. After I started taking this product, I was able to get off a hormonal medication I had been on for years. Elated by my results, I started looking into the company. What I discovered intrigued me. The CEO was a believer and one of the major drives of the company was raising money to provide immune support supplements to children with compromised health, most of whom were in orphanages. It was not just a business, but a cause I believed in and wanted to be a part of. I prayed and talked it over with my husband before making the decision to get involved. I had never done this type of business before, but it seemed like a perfect fit for me, and I went all in.

In the beginning, I was working really hard and also really enjoying myself. The business grew very fast and the rapid growth was nothing short of a miracle. In just seven short months, I made it to the top level of the company. I was completely overwhelmed with gratitude for God's undeniable favor and blessing.

As time went on, I began focusing more and more on my business rather than the truly important aspects of my life. As a result, my relationship with the Lord began to suffer, and my heart became less and less tender toward the things of God. I was so caught up with all I had on my plate, I did not even realize it. You would think with all of the success I was experiencing, I would be ecstatic, but instead I was depressed. I compared my life to those around me, and all I could see were the things I felt I'd missed out on in life.

Sometimes great success has a way of exposing the worst in us, even more than great loss. I began to question everything I had built my life on. I was disappointed with where I was in my life, and I was disappointed with God.

Downward Spiral

In 2005, Hurricane Katrina hit New Orleans, my hometown of Mandeville, and all of the surrounding areas. Life came to a halt for everyone, and we were all merely in survival mode. People could hardly handle taking care of basic needs, much less building a business. Many livelihoods were affected and people could not afford to stay on these supplements any longer. With everything that had happened, I was not only emotionally and physically exhausted, but also at the point of a complete breakdown.

Every area of my life felt like it was falling apart. My business was failing from the devastating effects of Katrina. I was hurt and disappointed with God. And more than anything, I was disappointed with myself. In the beginning, I thought this business would be the answer for many unfulfilled dreams. Most of all, I believed it would open a door to the ministry I felt called to, and now everything was crumbling around me. On top of all that, the products had stopped working for me, and my hormone issues had come back. I had no desire to promote something I didn't believe in anymore, so I just quit.

A few months after I stopped building that business, I got involved in another company that seemed promising. I also went to real estate school and got my real estate license. I had made the decision to make my dreams happen, with or without God's help.

After all the time and work I invested to get my real estate license, I realized my heart just wasn't in it. That pursuit was put on pause, and I decided to quit the new business I had just gotten involved in. At this point, I was even more emotionally and physically exhausted, and I was also hurting, angry and confused.

Kentwood

During this dark season of my life, I decided to take a drive to visit my friend Kathy, who I had met through my first business. She owned and operated her family's dairy farm out in Kentwood, Louisiana, about an hour or so from my hometown. I always found solace out at Ms. Kathy's home in the country, and she felt like a safe place to me.

I opened up my heart on this particular visit and told her, "Right now I feel like a ship in the middle of the sea being tossed for all I'm worth." She listened to me intently and after a few minutes, she excused herself to go get something. When she came back, she was carrying a CD she had recorded years earlier with her band. She said,

"Let me play you a song." She put in the CD, and the song that played was the "The Anchor Holds" by Ray Boltz.[1] Tears began to stream down my face as I heard God's voice speak to my spirit. He told me that *my anchor would indeed hold.*

Finally Done

Even after my visit with Ms. Kathy, there was still no relief from the feeling of being in a great storm. For months I cried every day. I felt so broken and miserable and so far from the God I had once loved. I had to choose every day, sometimes many times a day, just to stay on the planet. If I could have pushed a button and disappeared, I would have. As much as I did not want to be alive, I knew I could not take my life.

By this time, my health was really suffering due to the constant stress of burning my candle at both ends. I was completely broken, and I hated where my heart was. I had finally come to the end of myself, and the options before me were clear: I could run away from my family, abandon my faith, and make some very unwise choices, or I could turn and seek God with all of my heart. After all, where was I going to go? I knew only Jesus had the words of eternal life, so I set my heart to seek God.

Chapter 3

His Redeeming Love

After hitting rock bottom, I knew what I had to do. I began to get up every morning determined to make seeking God the most important thing I would do that day. This was not a place of casual desire, but one of determined desperation. I went after God as if my life depended on it, and I now know that it absolutely did.

> *And you will seek Me and find Me, when you search for Me with all your heart. I will be found by you, says the Lord, and I will bring you back from your captivity (Jeremiah 29:13–14 NKJV).*

It was late summer of 2006, almost one year after Katrina hit our town, when I felt the Holy Spirit drawing me out to the lakefront (an area close to my home in Mandeville, right by Lake Pontchartrain). Every morning I went to the lakefront with my heart and my Bible, asking God to speak to me. After several weeks of seeking Him, I heard nothing, and I felt just as far away as I did when I started. I was becoming more and more desperate for a breakthrough, and I knew I would not stop until I got one.

Unconditional Pursuit

During this time, the Holy Spirit brought to mind a book I was given, but had yet to read, called *Redeeming Love* by Francine Rivers. *Redeeming Love* is a fiction novel inspired by a story in the Bible from the book of Hosea.[1] In the biblical story, Hosea is a righteous man who marries a prostitute named Gomer out of obedience to what the Lord spoke to him. Even though Gomer is married to a good man, she keeps going back to the arms of her other lovers. In Hosea chapter two, God tells Hosea to love his wife, in spite of her continual adultery. Hosea continues to pursue Gomer and determines to bring her back into relationship by showing her total, unconditional love, even when she does not deserve it.

God's timing was perfect. The Holy Spirit knew the exact moment I needed to read this book. Reading *Redeeming Love* softened my heart in ways I could not have imagined, and it spoke volumes to me of God's pure, unconditional love.

Back to My First Love

I was familiar with the book of Hosea, but I felt the Holy Spirit drawing me to read it again right after I finished reading *Redeeming Love*. As I began to read about Gomer in chapter two of Hosea, I saw myself.

And she shall follow after her lovers but she shall not overtake
them; and she shall seek them [inquiring for and requiring them],
but shall not find them (Hosea 2:7 AMPC).

I too had played the harlot, running after other "lovers" to fulfill me.
My other lovers weren't bad things. They were just things, even
good things. First I thought if I got married I would be happy. Then I
thought if I could just have children. Then it became the house I so
desperately wanted and thought I needed. Or maybe if I could just
become a successful business woman and have a ministry, then I
would be fulfilled. Everything I had been denied in childhood, and
even as an adult, I tried to get for myself. And yet, the more I went
after those things, the more miserable I became.

Then shall she say, Let me go and return to my first husband, for
then was it better with me than now (Hosea 2:7 AMPC).

I felt the Lord's sweetness calling me back to my first love, back to a
place that was much better than the place I was now. It was God's
tender mercy that had kept me from finding fulfillment in my other
loves. Yes, there was some satisfaction, but ultimately my other
loves would disappoint time and time again, and they could
somehow never be quenched. Next, I went on to read Hosea 2:14–
15, where He speaks:

Therefore, behold, I will allure her [Israel] and bring her into the
wilderness, and I will speak tenderly and to her heart. There I will
give her her vineyards and make the Valley of Achor [troubling] to
be for her a door of hope and expectation (AMPC).

In this verse, God is addressing Israel, but as I read these words, He was speaking directly to my heart. He revealed that He had allowed me to go through this dark night of the soul in order to bring me to the absolute end of myself. Then He told me this was the very thing I had needed, and it had brought me to the place where He could open a door of hope into my soul. He was calling me into the wilderness to completely redeem me. He not only wanted to take me back to the love I had known in the beginning, but He also wanted to take me somewhere I had never gone before.

Just like God gave Israel her vineyards, the thing she had wanted, I too got what I thought I wanted. By making it to the top level in my company, I thought I had really accomplished something, but ultimately it became a place of great disappointment.

An Invitation

And it shall be in that day, says the Lord, that you will call Me Ishi [my Husband], and you shall no more call Me Baali [my Baal] (Hosea 2:16 AMPC).

Jesus was inviting me to a new level of surrender beyond anything I had ever known. He did not want to be my master anymore; He was inviting me into complete union. Marriage would mean I had to let Him love me, really love me, even with all of the things I knew were still wrong with me.

I had been a Christian since I was fourteen, but for the very first time, I saw that there were parts of my heart I had not surrendered. I saw a pattern in my life where I had been afraid to give God complete control. Something inside had kept me from being able to totally let go and just trust in His goodness. I began to see how I'd believed the same lie Eve believed in the garden. I had a deep-seated fear that Jesus might somehow be holding out on me. In my mind I told myself I trusted Him, but had I?

True Surrender

Reading *Redeeming Love* and the book of Hosea opened my eyes to see how Jesus had been passionately pursuing my heart since I became a believer. His loving kindness brought me to a place of deep repentance, and I was finally able to let go. I agreed to let Him in every room of my heart and to love the parts even I couldn't love. I surrendered to His love and said, "Yes, I will marry you."

When I said yes, I heard Jesus speak these words to my heart: "You've been running all of your life, but I have finally caught you." I honestly had no idea until then that I had been running, but I felt so relieved to finally be done.

Before this, if someone asked if I had surrendered my life to Jesus, I would have said, "I have led Bible studies and served in youth and women's ministry. I read my Bible, pray fervently, and have loved Jesus passionately in most seasons of my life. Of course I'm surrendered!" But something inside of me had rejected His love. There had been a wall preventing me from totally letting go. My wall was the belief that it wasn't okay to be loved with so many issues. The only time I felt worthy of love was when I performed well. This meant most of the time I felt rejected, even by God. This came from my very deep-seated belief system that to be loved, I had to be perfect. In my head I knew Jesus made me worthy, but until I radically experienced His unconditional love and pursuit, my heart did not fully believe it.

In the moment I said yes and totally surrendered, something divine took place on the inside of me, and I knew I would never be the same again. Before this, I had struggled to feel worthy of His love, but after this, I began to see myself totally loved and everything in my life started to change. He poured out His love in such a manifest way, and I was so overwhelmed that all I could do was cry. This went on for weeks and weeks. I just sat in the presence of God, and I wept. It was like nothing I had ever known. I could feel His love going into the deepest places inside of me. He was healing my broken heart. For the first time, I knew Him in total union. He was mine, and I was His. He loved me unconditionally, and there was nothing I could do that would change that.

New Freedom

For I will take away the names of Baalim [the Baals] out of her mouth, and they shall no more be mentioned or seriously remembered by their name (Hosea 2:17 AMPC).

Baals represent other gods or things that have mastered us. From my story, you already know the thing that had mastered my life was my eating disorder, but this scripture is also referring to anything that ruled my life as a believer other than Jesus. It was a promise that through our union, everything else that ruled in my life would be taken away. He would take them so far away that they would be totally forgotten. So far away that they would never be mentioned ever again. This was beyond anything I could imagine, and it seemed too good to be true.

*And in that day will I make a covenant for Israel . . . I will break the bow and the sword and [abolish battle equipment and] conflict out of the land and will make you lie down safely (*Hosea 2:18 AMPC).*

Just like God made a covenant with Israel, Jesus had made a covenant with me, and with this covenant, He was taking away the things I had battled all of my life. Not only would I not have to battle, but those things would also not be a temptation anymore. The constant struggle ceased, and for the first time, I knew what it was like to have quiet in my mind and true peace in my heart. I could now rest from the weariness of being in a constant battle. Before this, I always had to try so hard, but now it was just easy.

A Wedding Gift

And I will betroth you to Me forever; yes, I will betroth you to Me in righteousness and justice, in steadfast love, and in mercy (Hosea 2:19 AMPC).

I was no longer striving to become righteous because my union with Jesus had changed everything. I had always believed I was righteous based on the work of the cross, but it was not until I received Him through total union that I experienced it. My marriage to Him came with a beautiful wedding gift of righteousness. The inward righteousness and holiness I was experiencing was something I had only dreamed about, but never knew really existed on this side of heaven. The inward struggle of trying to be good was gone. I was good because I was His.

Worth the Wait

As I consumed this chapter from Hosea, God unraveled my whole life before me. He opened my eyes to the journey I had been on that led me to this place of complete surrender. He showed me a time in my life, many years after I had become a believer, when I was unable to surrender what He asked me. All of those years I carried so much guilt because I felt like I missed my opportunity. Jesus told me He knew all along that I would not be ready then, and I was already completely forgiven for turning Him down at that point in my life. He knew the exact moment I would finally say yes to His love and hold nothing back. He told me He had been waiting, and I had been worth the wait. To experience this kind of love wrecked me from the inside out, and I knew I would never be able to return to life as it had been before. I was now His totally devoted bride, and I would never get over His passionate pursuit of my hand in marriage.

I will even betroth you to Me in stability and in faithfulness, and you shall know (recognize, be acquainted with, appreciate, give heed to, and cherish) the Lord (Hosea 2:20 AMPC).

Chapter 4

When I Said Yes

W hen I said yes and married Jesus on the altar of my heart, He lifted my veil and kissed me. We came face to face, and for the first time, I could see Him clearly. His kiss awakened my heart. My sleep had been induced over time as a result of biting into the bitter fruit of religion and listening to another voice rather than my Good Shepherd.

> *Draw me into your heart. We will run away together into the king's cloud-filled chamber (Song of Songs 1:4 TPT).*

Jesus was not only calling me higher, but He was also calling me deeper than I had ever been before. Once I let Him into all of the rooms of my heart, His desire was to take me to a deeper level of union.

Song of Songs

After saying yes to marriage, the Holy Spirit led me to start reading the Song of Songs. For years I had only read this book on occasion, and I had been taught to believe it was about married love and passion, when in fact, the Song of Songs is God's love story between Christ and His bride. It is the story of her purification process to become a mature bride.

This purification process would begin in chapter one of the Song of Songs, where my journey into deeper union and purification would come not by doing, but simply by yielding. My bridegroom was asking me to yield and *let Him*. It wasn't about how hard I could try anymore. All I had to do was yield. I was the responder; Jesus was the initiator.

When I read chapter one in the Song of Songs, I could feel His love overtaking my heart as I read the words of love written to me, His bride. He began to affirm me through words of love, telling me in chapter one and then in chapter two, just how beautiful I was to Him. Even with things in my life that were dark, He saw me as completely pure. As the Alpha and Omega, He already saw me as a mature bride, even though I still felt unworthy of such incredible love.

His love began to break through all of my barriers and the places I hid from Him in shame. As I continued on in chapter one, I saw my journey out of shame and into the light of His great love for me. I was totally caught up in this great love affair, just enjoying the sweetness, but now He wanted to start dealing with the areas of my life that still needed healing.

Catching the Foxes

You must catch the troubling foxes, those sly little foxes that hinder our relationship. For they raid our budding vineyard of love to ruin what I've planted within you. Will you catch them and remove them for me? We will do it together (Song of Songs 2:15 TPT).

The little foxes represent the areas of our lives that have not been transformed by the Holy Spirit. Jesus was asking me if I was ready to go further and deeper into the areas He wanted me to have freedom. Areas I didn't even know I had when He asked me this question.

Like the Shulamite woman in chapter two, I was not sure if I was really ready for that next level of heart purity. I was still basking in my freedom from years of struggling with an eating disorder. What more could He want? Couldn't I just have a little time to enjoy this? I thought if I could just get through that battle, I would have it "made in the shade." I could not have been more wrong.

My Turn to Pursue

Like the Shulamite bride, sometimes I was not ready to deal with something the Holy Spirit was bringing to the surface. I did not say no, but in my fear, I hesitated and grieved the Holy Spirit. Then I experienced what the Shulamite bride did in chapter two, when she does not follow Jesus to the Mountains of Separation, and He goes on without her.

Night after night I'm tossing and turning on my bed of travail. Why did I let him go from me? How my heart now aches for him, but he

is nowhere to be found! So I must rise in search of him, looking
throughout the city, seeking until I find him. Even if I have to roam
through every street, nothing will keep me from my search (Song of
Songs 3:1–2 TPT).

Jesus never forces us to follow where He is leading, but He will continue on without us if we choose not to come with Him. Pursuing Him back in these moments is often part of the process of growing us into maturity. Before surrendering to marriage, there were times of separation, and it felt normal, but now I could not live disconnected from Jesus. Whenever I felt disconnected, I began to desperately search for Him.

Just as I moved past them, I encountered him. I found the one I
adore! I caught him and fastened myself to him, refusing to be
feeble in my heart again (Song of Songs 3:4 TPT).

Like the Shulamite woman, I too wondered how I could possibly let Him go, for my heart now ached for Him like never before. I would no longer let time pass before I found Him again and fastened my heart. Something had changed inside of me at this point. I would follow the Lord wherever He was asking me to go, even if it meant new realms of holiness and purity. I could not let Him go without me. I was now willing to lay down anything that held me back.

Washed by His Word

After the Shulamite bride found her beloved again, she stayed in constant connection and grew in her depth of the Word of God. And just like her, so did I. I spent tons of time feasting on the Word of God, allowing it to cleanse me in the inner recesses of my heart.

When I look at you, I see how you have taken my fruit and tasted my word. Your life has become clean and pure, like a lamb washed and newly shorn. You now show grace and balance with truth on display (Song of Songs 4:2 TPT).

As I continued to feast on the Word of God, I was being changed into a totally different person.

When I look at you, I see your inner strength, so stately and strong. You are as secure as David's fortress. Your virtues and grace cause a thousand famous soldiers to surrender to your beauty (Song of Songs 4:4 TPT).

In the Song of Songs, I received the words of love, affirmation, and encouragement my heart needed from my bridegroom king. He was always telling me what was right about my life rather than what was wrong. He pulled out the gold in me with His words, and the Holy Spirit started to teach me how to nurture others with my words as well.

Suffering Love

After I had grown in my level of purity, and I had matured in my walk with the Lord, I was ready to say yes when He asked me to go with Him to the mountain top, the Mountain of Suffering Love.

I've made up my mind. Until the darkness disappears and the dawn has fully come, in spite of shadows and fears, I will go to the mountaintop with you—the mountain of suffering love and the hill of burning incense. Yes, I will be your bride (Song of Songs 4:6 TPT).

This is where I experienced a huge transition in my life and my walk with God. I call it the place of no return. What I mean by this statement is that I believe once someone is willing to become one with Christ in His sufferings, they will never be able to turn back from following Him. This is the place of no return. Everything changes from that point on, and your life becomes a place of settled security.

> *And I continually long to know the wonders of Jesus and to experience the overflowing power of his resurrection working in me. I will be one with him in his sufferings and become like him in his death. Only then will I be able to experience complete oneness with him in his resurrection from the realm of death (Philippians 3:10–11 TPT).*

This scripture describes the work God does inside of us as we yield to suffering. To be totally one with Christ, we must willingly suffer with Him. When we say yes to this path, it is something we do willingly. We yield even when it hurts. We worship in the middle of the pain, knowing that to suffer with Him and go through the same experiences, is a privilege and part of being one with Him. It is when we die to our own agenda and say, "Not my will, but yours be done" (Luke 22:42 NIV). We choose to die to what we want for the sake of obedience. Christ did this for us, and now we become one with Him as we suffer as He did.

> *And being found in appearance as a man, He humbled Himself and became obedient to the point of death, even the death of the cross (Philippians 2:8 NKJV).*

We all want to reign with Jesus, but scripture tells us this is only possible if we are willing to suffer with Him.

*You can trust these words: If we were joined with him in his death,
then we are joined with him in his life! If we are joined with him in
his sufferings, then we will reign together with him in his triumph
(2 Timothy 2:11–12 TPT).*

Being willing to embrace suffering was a big part of my maturing
process. When I was going through suffering, the Holy Spirit
revealed to me that during this time, if I would worship, God would
build His house inside of me, and this is exactly what happened.

*My darling bride, my private paradise, fastened to my heart. A
secret spring that no one else can have are you—my bubbling
fountain hidden from public view. What a perfect partner to me
now that I have you. Your inward life is now sprouting, bringing
forth fruit. What a beautiful paradise unfolds within you (Song of
Songs 4:12–14 TPT).*

We actually become a private paradise for our bridegroom as a result
of going through this process. His desire is that we become a suitable
partner. His Promised Land started to flow inside of me after I willingly went to the Mount of Suffering Love. After this, my love
became even greater and my union deeper than I had ever dreamed
possible. I found that my very thoughts were His thoughts. This is
the same union Jesus experienced with the Father. He was in such
deep union that He knew His Father's thoughts, and He simply did
what He heard the Father say and do.

Simply Irresistible

In chapter five, the bridegroom begins to feed Himself from the fruit
within the paradise garden of the bride's heart.

I have gathered from your heart, my equal, my bride . . . all the fruits of my life I have gathered from within you, my paradise garden. Come, all my friends—feast upon my bride, all you revelers of my palace. . . . Drink the wine of her love. Take all you desire . . . My life within her will become your feast (Song of Songs 5:1 TPT).

The bridegroom is so thrilled with His bride that He wants to show her off to His other lovers who are starting to awaken. At that moment, she is content in His love for her, but she soon grows apathetic and allows her devotion to slumber. I know this can happen to the best of us if we aren't careful. It's so easy to become satisfied with all He has done in our lives and want to just take a break.

Just when she decides she needs to rest, the bridegroom comes to her in the dark of night to ask her to go even further with Him, back to the Mount of Suffering Love. Again she hesitates, and then when she goes to respond, she realizes He has gone on without her, and she cannot find Him anywhere.

As I walked throughout the city in search of him, the overseers stopped me as they made their rounds. They beat me and bruised me until I could take no more. They wounded me deeply and removed my covering from me (Song of Songs 5:7 TPT).

In her search for her beloved, she experiences wounds from the overseers, who likely represent spiritual leaders. Unfortunately, this is a familiar scenario to so many people. Being hurt by spiritual authority can be so devastating, but it is how we handle it that tells the real story. The Shulamite Bride's response to being hurt is:

Nevertheless, make me this promise, you brides-to-be: if you find my beloved one, please tell him I endured all travails for him. I've been pierced through by love, and I will not be turned aside! (Song of Songs 5:8 TPT)

What love and devotion! Nothing else mattered to her, not even the hurt she endured. Devotion like this has the power to awaken others. When those around you see that no matter what you go through, you still love Jesus, they will want to know what makes Him so special, and they will want to know Him too. The most powerful form of evangelism is a yielded life. People will actually smell the fragrance of our devotion, want to be near us, and then wonder about this God we worship.

Overcome by the Bride

O my beloved, you are lovely. When I see you in your beauty, I see a radiant city where we will dwell as one. More pleasing than any pleasure, more delightful than any delight, you have ravished my heart, stealing away my strength to resist you (Song of Songs 6:4 TPT).

When the bride gets to this place in her life, it is because she and the bridegroom are fully one! Can you imagine coming to a place in your walk with Jesus where He is so overcome by your love for Him that He cannot resist you? What an incredible picture of divine romance. Coming into this kind of love and union brings to mind this verse:

But if you live in life-union with me and if my words live powerfully within you—then you can ask whatever you desire and it will be done (John 15:7 TPT).

The King cannot resist you. Do you think this could be a key to answered prayer? He becomes so overcome by our love for Him that He wants to answer the desires of our heart? I believe King David understood this kind of devotion when he wrote these words.

Take delight in the Lord, and he will give you your heart's desires (Psalms 37:4 NLT).

Joining the Dance

In chapter six, the bridegroom king continues to be completely overcome by his Shulamite bride. She is so beautiful that the brides-to-be actually sing of her beauty. At the end of the chapter, she is with the bridegroom, and this is what the Zion Maidens have to say to her:

Zion Maidens, Brides-to-Be
Come back! Return to us, O maiden of his majesty.
Dance for us as we gaze upon your beauty.

The Shulamite Bride
Why would you seek a mere Shulamite like me?
Why would you want to see my dance of love?

The Bridegroom-King
Because you dance so gracefully,
as though you danced with angels!
(Song of Songs 6:13 TPT)

Our lives become more and more beautiful as a result of marriage to our King, so much so that others want to watch the dance and join in too! Maybe the reason we have not seen the world come to Christ is because so few have actually married the King and had their lives transformed from the inside out. Christ wants others to see our dance of love. He wants them to be so jealous of our relationship with our King that they want to join the dance too!

We say we want revival, but what if what we really need is not just revival, but reformation? Maybe the road to reformation is marriage. Is this what the world is waiting for? Will the brides-to-be awaken when they see a purified bride in all her beauty? I believe this is what chapters six and seven of the Song of Songs are expressing.

> *Out of your innermost being is flowing the fullness of my Spirit— never failing to satisfy. Within your womb there is a birthing of harvest wheat; they are the sons and daughters nurtured by the purity you impart (Song of Songs 7:2–3 TPT).*

The harvest was within the bride's womb just waiting to come forth. We pray for the harvest to come, yet the harvest is within the bride. She had to come to a place of maturity so that children could first be conceived and then be delivered and come forth. This is us. We are the bride, and the harvest is within our wombs! God is waiting on us to marry Him and bring forth fruit.

Awakening the Sleeping Ones

In the next few verses, Jesus expresses delight in His bride. He tells her it is time for Him to take hold of her with His power because she has allowed Him to possess every part of her. He then says that her kisses of love will awaken those who are still asleep. This just amazes me. We want to know how to win the world to Jesus, and we find the answer right here in the seventh chapter of the Song of Songs.

The Bridegroom King

Your kisses of love are exhilarating,
more than any delight I've known before.
Your kisses of love awaken even the lips of sleeping ones.

The Shulamite Bride

Now I know that I am filled with my beloved
and all his desire are fulfilled in me.
Come away, my lover.
Come with me to the far away fields.
We will run away together to the forgotten places
and show them redeeming love.
Let us arise and run to the vineyards of your people
and see if the budding vines of love are now in full bloom.
We will discover if their passion is awakened.
There I will display my love for you.
(Song of Songs 7:9–12 TPT)

Those who are still asleep spiritually will see His love for us, and our love for Him, and *this* is what will awaken the world. Truly they will know we are Christians by our love (John 13:35). This divine romance will make those who are still asleep long for love.

Consumed by Love

As we step into chapter eight of the song of Songs, we find a fully mature bride who cannot be turned back from following her bridegroom no matter what she goes through. She has a seal of love over her heart, and her love for Him is now stronger than even death.

Rivers of pain and persecution will never extinguish this flame. Endless floods will be unable to quench this raging fire that burns within you. Everything will be consumed. It will stop at nothing as you yield everything to this furious fire until it won't even seem to you like a sacrifice anymore (Song of Songs 8:7 TPT).

This is the kind of love I think about when I hear stories of Christians in the Middle East and Africa, where they have been tortured, or watched loved ones tortured, and yet they have not denied Jesus. They have a love that has been tested even in the face of death.

Forever One

We will dance in the high place of the sky, yes, on the mountains of fragrant spice. Forever we shall be united as one! (Song of Songs 8:14 TPT)

At the end of the chapter, and the book of Song of Songs, the fully mature bride brings her bridegroom king total bliss. They are totally one together in the garden of her heart, and she has given Him everything. All she thinks about is hearing His voice and dancing with Him in a divine duet, as they will be forever united as one.

Chapter 5

Identity and Authority

Traditionally, when a bride marries, she receives a new name. Our name has so much importance to our identity. Being called by name makes us feel seen and known because it calls out who we are. Our name carries not only our identity, but also our history. When I completely surrendered to the Lord in marriage, I heard the Holy Spirit tell me I would receive a new name. I had read the scripture that referenced being given a new name before, but I never connected the dots to marriage until then.

Anyone with ears to hear must listen to the Spirit and understand what he is saying to the churches. To everyone who is victorious I will give some of the manna that has been hidden away in heaven. And I will give to each one a white stone, and on the stone will be engraved a new name that no one understands except the one who receives it (Revelations 2:17 NLT).

A new name comes with the territory of being married. As the veil is lifted, we gain a deeper revelation of His Word, which is the hidden manna from Heaven. The white stone represents what happens in the spirit realm, when we are given a new name from God. This is a very personal and special exchange that takes place as a result of union with Him.

New Identity

You [Judah] shall no more be termed Forsaken, nor shall your land be called Desolate any more. But you shall be called Hephz-ibah [My delight is in her], and your land be called Beulah [mar-ried]; for the Lord delights in you, and your land shall be married [owned and protected by the Lord] (Isaiah 62:4 AMPC).

Marriage to Jesus not only changed my whole life, but I also received a new name from Yahweh Himself. No longer the *aban-doned one,* I now saw myself as *His delight.* When I came into my true identity as His bride, I knew without a shadow of a doubt that I was His beloved.

According to this verse in Isaiah, I am also the land He marries and redeems. Yes, God calls us His land. We are the land that He has purchased back from the enemy. Our bride-price was His very own blood, and we represent the ground He has taken back from the enemy and conquered through love.

Chosen and Pursued

But now, this is what the Lord says—he who created you, Jacob, he who formed you, Israel: "Do not fear, for I have redeemed you; I have summoned you by name; you are mine" (Isaiah 43:1 NIV).

He chose me before I had even met Him, and He longed for more of me when my heart had yet to completely surrender. He never gave up the pursuit until He had captured my heart, and I abandoned myself to His love. He had summoned me by name, and He wanted me. I was no longer rejected, but chosen. There is something so life changing about being identified as *chosen*. As a teenager, I felt like I had chosen Jesus, but the truth is He chose me. Jesus relentlessly pursued me even in my brokenness, and this is what opened my eyes to how truly valuable I was to Him. He refused to give up on me, and He called me lovely even when I was still in so much bondage.

The Shulamite
I feel as dark and dry as the desert tents
of the wandering nomads.

The Shepherd-King
Yet you are so lovely—
like the fine linen tapestry hanging in the Holy Place.
(Song of Songs 1:5 TPT)

Like the Shulamite bride, how Jesus felt about me was very different from how I felt about myself. I saw myself as flawed and broken, but He saw me already purified and complete in Him. This was my true identity, but I had not been able to take hold of the truth about myself until Jesus began to affirm me by telling me who I was. He did this over and over, until I began to believe what He said instead of the perceptions I had about myself.

After I surrendered to marriage, I was now completely His, and my life would never belong to another. My old identity and how I saw myself had been totally cut away. I was no longer tied to my past or the guilt I carried from failures I experienced in my walk with God.

> *Through our union with him we have experienced circumcision of heart. All of the guilt and power of sin has been cut away and is now extinct because of what Christ, the Anointed One, has accomplished for us (Colossians 2:11 TPT).*

With my new name and my new identity, I felt secure in His love for the first time. My life disappeared inside of His love, and the old me could not be found. He hid me in the secret place of His heart, and fear of the future began to lose its grip in the light of His faithfulness.

> *So it is impossible for God to lie for we know that his promise and his vow will never change! And now we have run into his heart to hide ourselves in his faithfulness (Hebrews 6:18 TPT).*

An Intimate Friend

When I married Jesus, my identity became not only His bride, but also His friend. I was no longer just a servant in His house.

> *You are my friends if you keep on doing what I command you. I do not call you servants any longer, for the servant does not know*

*what his master is doing; but I have called you [My] friends,
because I have revealed to you everything that I have heard from
My Father (John 15:14–15 AMP).*

As His friend, I was able to see and hear in the kingdom realm like I
never had before. The Holy Spirit began to show me the importance
of my dreams and how God wanted to speak to me through them.
Not only did I begin to hear with more clarity in my spirit, but God
gave me visions as well. I learned to tune my ear to Him and ask
what He wanted to show me when this happened. As a friend, He
began to share His secrets with me and what was on His mind. The
following is just a brief window into one of our conversations.

One day, I was painting a piece of furniture, and I heard the Holy
Spirit say, "Pain killers." Then He began to quote Isaiah chapter 61
to me.

*The Spirit of the Lord God is upon me, because the Lord has
anointed and qualified me to preach the Gospel of good tidings to
the meek, the poor, and afflicted; He has sent me to bind up and
heal the brokenhearted, to proclaim liberty to the [physical and
spiritual] captives and the opening of the prison and of the eyes to
those who are bound (Isaiah 61:1–3 AMPC).*

After this, He told me: "Pain killers make people sleepy. I want to
heal people's heart pain so they can get off pain killers. When their
hearts are healed, they will get off pain killers and awaken spiritually." I just sat there on the floor of my room dialoguing with God, and
He began to show me all of the different pain killers people were
using. I saw visions and heard Him say, "These are things my children are using as pain killers: sex, drugs, alcohol, sports, hobbies,

shopping, food, porn, work, and so forth. It's anything they use to make themselves feel better that is not from me, even ministry or good works if I'm not in it. These are numbing agents to avoid pain, and all of these pain killers have put them to sleep spiritually."

I lived in conversations like these on a constant basis, as Jesus shared His heart with me, just like I would share my heart with an intimate friend.

Answered Prayer

There's a private place reserved for the devoted lovers of Yahweh, where they sit near him and receive the revelation-secrets of his promises (Psalms 25:14 TPT).

As I grew more intimate in my friendship with Jesus, I heard His voice more and more clearly, and my prayers were answered like never before. This happened especially when it came to those closest to my heart—my children. Jesus would often bring different scriptures to mind that I would then meditate on and pray over them. It was not me searching for a verse to pray, but Him quickening them to my spirit. Because I was praying His words, I knew I was praying His heart for them, and I saw miraculous turnarounds, often in just a short amount of time. Prayer being answered was the fruit that came from my union with Him. Jesus gave me His words, and I began to experience John chapter 15.

But if you live in life-union with me and if my words live powerfully within you—then you can ask whatever you desire and it will be done (John 15:7 TPT).

The Awakened Bride of Christ

When I married the Lord, I became part of a company of people whose every breath was for Him alone. This group of people were easy to identify because of the love they carried for Jesus. After talking to them only a short time, I would recognize them by their speech. It was different. They all spoke the language of surrender, and they all carried a certain frequency of heaven. They were the awakened bride—the remnant.

> *In that day the Lord of hosts will be For a crown of glory and a diadem of beauty To the remnant of His people (Isaiah 28:5 NKJV).*

God always has a remnant, and they are those who have accepted the invitation to make Him their everything. They are not merely born again, but they have been separated and set apart for Him alone. All other pursuits take a backseat to pursuing Jesus, and they never cease from following Him, no matter the cost. The awakened bride is a laid down lover.

> *And I will make an everlasting covenant with them: I will never stop doing good for them. I will put a desire in their hearts to worship me, and they will never leave me (Jeremiah 32:40 NLT).*

I believe we are in a time when the window is open with an invitation to become His beloved bride. It is an invitation to come away with Him to the marriage chamber. I'm not sure what my life would look like if I had not responded to that invitation. I feel such an urgency about this in my spirit, for this day and this hour. I do believe it is possible to miss your day of visitation. In the parable about the ten virgins waiting for the bridegroom, not all of them were ready when the invitation came, and they missed the wedding feast.

"Then the kingdom of heaven will be like ten virgins, who took their lamps and went to meet the bridegroom. Five of them were foolish [thoughtless, silly, and careless], and five were wise [far-sighted, practical, and sensible]. For when the foolish took their lamps, they did not take any [extra] oil with them, but the wise took flasks of oil along with their lamps. Now while the bride-groom was delayed, they all began to nod off, and they fell asleep. But at midnight there was a shout, 'Look! The bride-groom [is coming]! Go out to meet him.' Then all those virgins got up and put their own lamps in order [trimmed the wicks and added oil and lit them]. But the foolish virgins said to the wise, 'Give us some of your oil, because our lamps are going out.' But the wise replied, 'No, otherwise there will not be enough for us and for you, too; go instead to the dealers and buy oil for your-selves.' But while they were going away to buy oil, the bride-groom came, and those who were ready went in with him to the wedding feast; and the door was shut and locked. Later the others also came, and said, 'Lord, Lord, open [the door] for us.' But He replied, 'I assure you and most solemnly say to you, I do not know you [we have no relationship]'" (Mathew 25:1–12 AMP).

This might be one of the most sobering passages of scripture I know. When Jesus says, "I do not *know* you" in the last verse, He is refer-ring to the intimate knowledge you get only through experience with someone. I had been like one of the foolish virgins, and I was asleep with no oil to spare. After the Lord awakened me from my sleep with an intimate kiss, I knew I could never allow myself to slumber again.

The bride makes herself ready by saying yes and yielding over and over again. She continuously chooses Him and continues to yield to the purification process. She stays awake and does not allow herself to be lulled to sleep by the deception of the enemy.

> *I am jealous for you with a godly jealousy because I have promised you to one husband, to present you as a pure virgin to Christ. But I am afraid that, even as the serpent beguiled Eve by his cunning, your minds may be corrupted and led away from the simplicity of [your sincere and] pure devotion to Christ (2 Corinthians 11:2–3 AMP).*

The Power of Identity

The more solidified I became in my identity—as His beloved, as His friend, as the awakened bride—the more I grew in authority. I was becoming a mature bride who was now a wall of protection for others going on the same journey.

> *But now I have grown and become a bride, and my love for him has made me a tower of passion and contentment for my beloved. I am now a firm wall of protection for others, guarding them from harm (Song of Song 8:10 TPT).*

I grew as I yielded to Him and submitted myself to the purification process. I began to walk not only in my identity, but also in my authority, and this my friend, is what the enemy does not want for us. We can be wonderful, sweet Christians with a ticket to heaven all of our lives, but it's when we step into our authority and begin to take back the enemy's territory, that we become a threat to the kingdom of darkness.

> *Why would you bother with puny, mortal man or care about human beings? Yet what honor you have given to men, created only a little lower than Elohim, crowned with glory and magnificence. You have delegated to them rulership over all you have made, with everything under their authority, placing earth itself under the feet of your image-bearers. All the created order and every living thing of the earth, sky, and sea—the wildest beasts and all that move in the paths of the sea—everything is in submission to Adam's sons. (Psalms 8:4–8 TPT).*

Wow, is all I can say to this! As I meditated on these verses, I heard the Holy Spirit say to me, "He's jealous."

"What?" I said.

"The enemy is jealous of the sons of Adam. He hates the authority God has given you. His greatest threat is for you to actually discover the authority God intended you to walk in."

I began to see that God had actually given me authority in the areas I had conquered, and He wanted me to use it. Christ in me had brought victory to my life, and He wanted to express His authority through me. It was now time to allow Jesus to take back the ground the enemy had stolen in my family through my surrendered life.

Chapter 6

Transformed from the Inside Out

When I first gave my heart to Jesus at fourteen, I started going to a house church where there was a room full of hippies raising their hands, worshiping God to acoustic guitar music. The presence of God was so strong it was incredible. In this very non-religious, unstructured environment, I felt Jesus's unconditional love and acceptance. I wanted to bring all of my friends to church with me because I knew they would love it, and it would be so different from what they had experienced before. God was real, and His presence was tangible in this place.

Being in this environment was a wonderful start to my Christian experience. Legalism and performance would become a part of my life later, but they were not part of my early experience with God. It took me years to see that my core beliefs were rooted in performance, and this would not go away just because I had become a Christian.

My parents were thrilled about my salvation experience, but I couldn't blame them for being disappointed when I was still struggling with my eating disorder just as much as I was before I got saved. Although I was so happy just to know Jesus, I was still not free. I knew this wasn't His fault, so it must be mine. I figured I just needed to try harder. My focus turned from the simplicity of loving Jesus to striving for deliverance. This became the goal of my Christian life more than anything else, and I started to lose sight of my love for Jesus. As a result, my life began to spiral downward. I was never able to get completely set free from my eating disorder; I just got better at hiding it, and I struggled on and off with it for years.

I started to feel that even in Christian circles, looking good on the outside was all that mattered. It didn't seem like anyone really wanted to know what was going on inside of me. If I just pretended to be fine, everyone would be happy and a lot more comfortable. Church began to feel more like a showplace than a hospital. Years went by, and things were always the same no matter what church I was in. I loved the Lord, and I even experienced great times of intimacy and long periods of freedom, but deep down I still felt like it was all about performance.

Not long after I gave my heart to the Lord, my core beliefs started to manifest, even in my relationship with Jesus. I believed if I was doing good, then I had God's love and approval. If I was not doing good, He must be disappointed with me. I lived in this cycle for over thirty years.

What I later realized was that Jesus had come to rescue my heart in 2006 and reintroduce me to the same God I had experienced as a young believer. The God I met right before my fifteenth birthday was the same God I was coming home to once again. He had never changed. The only thing that changed was how I had come to perceive Him.

A New Paradigm

All those years, no matter what circle of Christianity I found myself in, I was led to believe that if I would just be obedient, my sin problem would be gone. As much as I tried, I just could not obey, and it was only a matter of time before I would fail again. Focusing on my ability to obey only led to more and more failure. I was absolutely sure that I knew and loved Jesus, but it was not until I gave Him my yes, married Him, and came into union, that I began to bear the spiritual fruit I had desired all of my Christian life. Just like there could be no fruit without union in the natural realm, the same applied to my spiritual life.

> *So you must remain in life-union with me, for I remain in life-union with you. For as a branch severed from the vine will not bear fruit, so your life will be fruitless unless you live your life intimately joined to mine (John 15:4 TPT).*

When I came into union with Jesus, obedience became easy.

> *Loving me empowers you to obey my commands (John 14:15 TPT).*

> *Through our union with him we have experienced circumcision of heart. All of the guilt and power of sin has been cut away and is now extinct because of what Christ, the Anointed One, has accomplished for us (Colossians 2:11 TPT).*

Union did in me what nothing else ever could. Now that I was totally His and He was mine, I saw the lasting inner transformation I had always wanted. I was undone by the love of Jesus on a daily basis, and my heart melted in the revelation of who He really was. All of my life I had been striving to obey so that I would be pleasing to God. What had happened to the Galatians is exactly what happened to me.

> *Let me put this question to you: How did your new life begin? Was it by working your heads off to please God? Or was it by responding to God's Message to you? Are you going to continue this craziness? For only crazy people would think they could complete by their own efforts what was begun by God. If you weren't smart enough or strong enough to begin it, how do you suppose you could perfect it? Did you go through this whole painful learning process for nothing? It is not yet a total loss, but it certainly will be if you keep this up! (Galatians 3:2–4 MSG)*

What God had started by His Spirit, He would finish. I now understood that purification was a process, and this process takes time. Oh, how I wish I had an older, seasoned believer to instruct me during those early years. Someone who would have told me to keep my eyes focused on Jesus and my connection with Him. Instead, I set out to overcome my sin by focusing on it. Victory over sin became my main goal. I learned the hard way that what you focus on grows. Instead of getting free, I got worse. I would eventually have some success through behavior modification, but this was not true inner freedom. It would take many years before I would return to the simplicity of focusing on Jesus alone and not trying to perfect myself by works of the flesh.

In the same way you received Jesus our Lord and Messiah by faith, continue your journey of faith, progressing further into your union with him! Your spiritual roots go deeply into his life as you are continually infused with strength, encouraged in every way. For you are established in the faith you have absorbed and enriched by your devotion to him! (Colossians 2:6–7 TPT)

Breaking Free from Religious Mindsets

As I came into freedom and rest, I ceased from my own works, and my faith began to work through love. I was no longer afraid of punishment because I knew I was perfectly loved. Perfect love drove the fear of punishment far from my heart.

Love never brings fear, for fear is always related to punishment. But love's perfection drives the fear of punishment far from our hearts. Whoever walks constantly afraid of punishment has not reached love's perfection (I John 4:18 TPT).

I found that I had to set a guard over my heart to protect me from the religious works mentality I had walked out of. Let me clarify what I mean when I use the terms *religious works mentality* or *religious spirit*. A religious spirit or religious works mentality is always focused on the outward appearance of things rather than the heart, and more on religious activity rather than relationship. Jesus rebuked the Pharisees and called them white-washed tombs because they looked good on the outside, but they carried no life and were full of dead men's bones.

I had no problem with truth that brought correction, but if it had the residue of religion, I wanted nothing to do with it. I had no desire to go back into the religious works mentality that held me in bondage for so long. Jesus preached a radical message with many hard truths, yet the broken were always drawn to Him. It was always the religious who rejected Him, for they were merely interested in the outward standards of holiness, but not the radical inward transformation Jesus was offering.

I had always been taught to judge a tree by the fruit it produced. When the freedom I was experiencing seemed too good to be true, I heard the Lord say to me, "Look at the fruit." The fruit was good. My life was more clean and pure living by connection than it had ever been when I was trying to live by rules and regulations. I had more joy, more peace, and more of every fruit of the spirit. I began to relax and trust in His goodness, and I stopped fearing that I might get deceived. This radical message of grace had liberated me from the inside out, and the fruit was pure and sweet.

My desire had completely shifted from doing the right thing for the approval of others, to doing it out of pure love for Him. One day, Jesus shined a light on my old mindset when He asked me, "How would your earthly husband feel if what you did for Him was out of performance or duty rather than love?" Jesus felt the same way, and what He wanted was not only my heart, but also my love and my passion. He knew love would be enough to work inside of me the changes we both desired. His love was enough to make me whole. I was exhausted from years of trying to change myself using outward standards. Now I was living from the inside, and my love and devotion had nothing to do with duty or a desire for approval. I knew I was loved, and I already had His approval. This was real freedom.

Giving Grace to Myself and Others

As His love began to change me, I was able to give myself and others grace. It was the revelation of God's grace that had given me power to finally walk free from my sin. Grace had not given me an excuse to sin, but it had given me the power to overcome it.

> *God will continually revitalize you, implanting within you the passion to do what pleases him (Philippians 2:13 TPT).*

This is the best description of grace. So many people misunderstand grace and believe it gives them a license to sin. Nothing could be farther from the truth. Grace actually empowers us to do God's will, to do what pleases Him. I did not earn grace by my good behavior; I received grace as a gift when I recognized my need for Him. His grace was a gift, and I could now give it to others because it had been freely given to me.

Grace is a hard concept for the human mind to fathom. Like God's love, it is so confounding because it cannot be earned. Take, for instance, the story of the prodigal son. When the son returned home after wasting his inheritance, the father didn't punish him, but instead gave him grace. He gave the prodigal son what he *did not* and *could not* earn. The father's lavish display of love was met with disdain by the older brother, who felt this wasn't fair and became deeply offended. Grace does not make sense to us until we too have received it.

I think we are really so afraid of grace because we fear people will abuse it. If it is *true grace*, just the opposite will happen. Grace has the power to change and heal us from the inside out. When we withhold grace from others, hoping it will change their behavior, it drives them away instead of releasing freedom. The power of sin is in *the law*, not grace.

> *Death gets its power to hurt from sin, and sin gets its power from the Law (1 Corinthians 15:56 GNT).*

When we die to the law (our old husband) and marry Christ, we will finally experience the freedom Jesus paid for.

> *So, my dear brothers and sisters, the same principle applies to your relationship with God. For you died to your first husband, the law, by being co-crucified with the body of the Messiah. So you are now free to "marry" another—the one who was raised from the dead so that you may now bear spiritual fruit for God (Romans 7:4 TPT).*

Once again, we must give Jesus our yes. We have been crucified with Christ, but to bear spiritual fruit for God we must marry Him. It's a two step process—death and then marriage. Death and marriage will break the power of sin in our lives. We have no need to be afraid of grace because it has always been more powerful than sin.

True Grace

When I experienced this completely new paradigm in my life, I knew this was how I was born to live. Jesus brought me back to the Father's house where I received grace and unconditional love. As a result, I came to a place of rest. When children grow up in a grace-filled environment full of unconditional love, they are at rest because they feel safe. They will seek to protect connection with their family, and they have no desire to rebel. This is what God is inviting us into.

We are now starting to receive a revelation of true grace through those who have embraced its message. There is a company of people who are not afraid of grace because they know it works. After years of striving and failing, they received the gift of grace and now walk in their true identity. Union with Jesus produces righteousness in their lives, and they no longer strive to "be good." They have come into a clear understanding that the only place we are encouraged to strive is to enter into His rest.

> *For whoever has entered God's rest has also rested from his works as God did from his. Let us therefore strive to enter that rest, so that no one may fall by the same sort of disobedience (Hebrews 4:10–11 ESV).*

Chapter 7

Coming Into His Rest

Before 2006, I believed I always needed to be doing something for God, but all of this began to change in the presence of divine love. He wanted me to know I couldn't *do* anything to make Him love me more. I was already loved. All He wanted was my heart. If I never did another thing in ministry, I would still be pleasing to Him. I realized I didn't need a ministry; I only needed Him.

Before I had this revelation, I was focused on what I needed to be doing for Him rather than on what He had done for me. One day, as I spent time in God's presence, I attempted to pray. I felt so guilty for sitting and enjoying Him and letting Him love me. Inside I sensed that all He wanted from me was to just sit quietly. This was so hard to do. During those quiet moments, Jesus spoke to my heart: "Kay, I am asking you to just be quiet. If your husband was trying to make love to you, and you just kept talking, he would want you to just shush. It's okay to sit in silence with me. I want you to just shush and let me love you."

When my children got older, they told me one of the things they remembered most about growing up was hearing me pray. In many seasons of my Christian walk, I prayed for an hour a day. I will never forget hearing Larry Lea's teaching about praying through the Lord's Prayer back in the eighties.[1] I prayed in the spirit until I felt the presence of God, and then I continued until I felt I had covered all of my bases. I believed I had to do something Pentecostals call "praying through." I had to know I had touched heaven, and in my mind, this meant I needed to feel a strong emotion, which usually included tears. As much as I love having this happen, I was beginning to understand that this was not the only way God moved or heard my prayers. I kept hearing the Holy Spirit tell me to just be quiet. At first I felt guilty, like I was doing something wrong, but I knew He was asking me to be still and know that He was God.

He says, "Be still, and know that I am God; I will be exalted among the nations, I will be exalted in the earth" (Psalms 46:10 NIV).

Be Still and Know

Being still and quiet in the presence of God still felt foreign. After years of feeling like I needed to be busy, this was hard for me to embrace. But the Holy Spirit began to teach me, and as I learned to become still, the tangible manifestation of His presence was doing more than I could put into words. I was so overwhelmed by what He was doing in me, and yet I still didn't fully understand. One day I asked Him, "What do you want me to do for you?" My whole walk with God had been built on what I needed to be doing *for Him* rather than on just being *with Him*.

As I continued to seek Him, all I heard as an answer to my question was, "I want you to be still and know that I am God." This was still such unfamiliar territory, and it felt totally unnatural. Christianity had always been about doing. I then asked the Lord if I should start a Bible study. This was something I had done in many seasons of my adult life, and this is what I thought He might have in mind. I wanted to get involved in ministry again and be doing something. My heart was so on fire, and I was so excited about the work He had started in my life. But, every time I asked, His still, small voice answered, "No, just be still and know that I am God."

Being involved in ministry often meant seeking God just to receive what I needed for a Bible study I was leading. Now I was spending loads of time in the Word of God and in His presence just to be with Him and get to know Him. I had no agenda. The only purpose was relationship. I started to put myself in the Lord's shoes. How would I have felt if someone I loved only spent time with me for what I could give and not simply for the pleasure of my company? What kind of relationship would that be? I let this sink in, and it spoke volumes to my heart. I realized how much our relationship had changed now that it wasn't about what He could give me or what He could do for me. I wanted to be with Him just to be with Him.

Not To Do but Just to Be

Even with everything the Holy Spirit was revealing to me, I still felt a tremendous amount of guilt over just being still and not doing anything. Everything in me told me I needed to be about my Father's business because that was what I had been taught my whole Christian life. When you got born again, the first goal was to get you cleaned up and then put you to work winning souls and making disciples, right? How could being still and knowing God possibly be all I was supposed to be doing at this time? So, I asked the Lord a third time about starting a Bible study, and this was His response: "You can do it if you want, but it will just be a work of the flesh to make you feel better about yourself." This time I knew I had my answer. If I started a Bible study, it wouldn't be out of obedience or a desire to please Him. This made me think about all of the things in my life that may have been good things, but were not necessarily God things. I was starting to understand what Jesus meant when He said, "I only do the works I see the father doing" (John 5:19 TPT).

After all of this, it still took everything in me to quiet the voice of condemnation telling me I wasn't doing anything for God. One day, as I was still struggling with this, I heard the Holy Spirit speak to my heart as clear as a bell, and I was given a little saying that goes like this: "Not to do, but just to be, is what the Lord requires of me." After this, the voice of condemnation lost its grip, and I was finally able to have some peace.

Lovers Make the Best Warriors

And from the days of John the Baptist until now the kingdom of heaven suffers violence, and the violent take it by force (Matthew 11:12 NKJV).

I grew up believing that I always had to be in warfare mode. Scriptures that taught about war, like the one above, were constantly being preached, and yet, no one ever seemed to talk about the rest of God. Warfare seemed to be the language of the "spiritually mature," and I came to believe that if I was not at war, something must be wrong with me.

There will always be a need to do warfare when God calls us to war, but God wanted to take me to a place of rest in my heart. As I stepped into this new season in my walk with God, I saw prayers answered, not from warring, but simply from trusting in His goodness. I knew it pleased Him for me to trust His character and believe that He loved me. Scriptures like this one began to jump off the page.

> *Surely goodness and mercy and unfailing love shall follow me all the days of my life, And I shall dwell forever . . . in the house and in the presence of the Lord (Psalms 23:6 AMP).*

King David was a lover. He rested in God's goodness, and He lived a life of continual worship. He showed us a beautiful picture of what we can walk in as a New Covenant believer. When I chose to worship rather than worry, my anxious heart was transformed, and my faith in God's character began to move the mountains I longed to see move in my life. It was so hard when I first started to do this. I had to choose worship rather than worry over and over again until it started to become my first response. I'm still learning to do this, and I think I always will be. Just because we know what we need to do, doesn't mean we have arrived.

A Great Reset Into Rest

> *As we enter into God's faith-rest life we cease from our own works, just as God celebrates his finished works and rests in them (Hebrews 4:10 TPT).*

To be still and rest is so hard for many Christians, but this can be especially true of those in ministry. It's easy to have the fear of missing out, the fear of losing a ministry, and even the fear of not being pleasing to God if we are not doing enough. Many have fallen into sin, or fallen away from their first love because of this drive to work for God. Their identity has become rooted in what they are doing for Him, and it becomes harder and harder to pull themselves away.

Many have called this the time "The Great Reset," and it seems to be exactly that. The lockdown from the pandemic caused many churches to be closed for a time, and many experienced a forced rest during this season. Although many have experienced great loss, God never wastes anything. He has been calling us back to our first love.

In his book *The Problem of Pain,* C.S. Lewis wrote, "God whispers to us in our pleasures, speaks in our conscience, but shouts in our pains: it is his megaphone to rouse a deaf world."[2] Maybe this has everything to do with what God is up to. We will only rest when we rest in Him and Him alone. Years ago, Bob Jones prophesied that we would come into His rest in the 2020s. He said:

> The 2020s will reveal the rest of God, where the body will come into a place of resting in God . . . and in this rest, the enemy will not be able to do warfare because we're resting in God, and He's resting in us. And He will accomplish the things He means to do in a people that's at rest. He has always wanted a people that would come into His rest. There never has been one, but it's on the way.[3]

Chapter 8

Cultivating and Protecting Connection

Every night before my husband and I go to bed, he puts his arm out so I can come close and he can hold me. We have been married forty-one years, and this has been a habit all of our married lives. It forces us to connect no matter what type of day we've had. It might be one of the biggest keys to still being happily married after all these years. We do exactly the same thing in the morning. This way, we connect before we get our day going. When you love someone, your heart desires connection as soon as you wake up!

I want the same kind of connection in my relationship with God, so I start my day with gratitude. It takes me right into His presence and right into connection.

Enter His gates with a song of thanksgiving And His courts with praise. Be thankful to Him, bless and praise His name (Psalms 100:4 AMP).

I start each day just thanking Him for who He is—for His loving kindness, His faithfulness, and His goodness in my life. I remind myself of all He has done for me and my family, and I thank Him. Even on days when I only have a few minutes to read my Bible, I can still soak in His presence through gratefulness. Gratitude always cultivates connection in any relationship.

My Daily Devotion

Every day I made a place for the Trinity in my life. When I say the Trinity, I mean God the Father, God the Son, and God the Holy Spirit. They are all God, but different expressions of Him. I cultivated my relationship with all three at different times and in different seasons.

In the beginning of my love story, it was all about Jesus. It was Jesus who came to me with His marriage proposal, and saying yes to marriage completely transformed our relationship. I would have visions of myself at the beach, walking along the edge of the water in a beautiful, white gown. Jesus would walk right behind me, and as we walked, He would gaze at me adoringly, like I was the only girl in the world. He was always smiling and playful when I was with Him, and I could feel how much He loved and enjoyed me.

For several years I developed my relationship with Jesus, and then my focus shifted to the person of the Holy Spirit. I found I could know the Holy Spirit in the same manner I could Jesus. The Holy Spirit had been in my life since I gave my heart to Christ, but this was different. Now there was a very focused attention on developing our relationship.

You can know someone as an acquaintance for a long time, but when you spend more time with them, the relationship usually goes to a new level of intimacy. This is what happened with the Holy Spirit. The more time we spent together, the more I got to know Him and became familiar with His likes and dislikes. I became more and more sensitive to His feelings, and I found that although He can be grieved, He can also feel great joy.

I remember one particular time when I learned this firsthand. Someone in my life was having a rough day, and their attitude was really affecting me. As I talked with the Holy Spirit, He prompted me to speak into the atmosphere and declare the opposite of what this person was projecting. I began to call things into existence with words of life, and when I did, I could feel the Holy Spirit jumping up and down on the inside. I knew I was on the right track, doing exactly what the Holy Spirit wanted me to do in that moment. Shortly after, this person's heart and demeanor totally changed. My intimate friendship with the Holy Spirit was better than being in the best Bible college, because there is no school like the school of the Holy Spirit. He is truly the best teacher I have ever known.

As my friendship with the Holy Spirit grew, I began to trust His ability to get to the bottom of every matter concerning me. The Holy Spirit became the counselor I relied on to reveal the hidden places of my heart and show me what needed to be transformed. He brought His light and the life-transforming truth I needed to restore me back to God's original intent.

> *And by the blood of his cross, everything in heaven and earth is brought back to himself—back to its original intent, restored to innocence again! (Colossians 1:20 TPT)*

My greatest pleasure in life became the intimate time I spent with Jesus and the Holy Spirit. Many days I had to pull myself away so I could get on with my day. When I was still working, I really had to prioritize to make this time happen. I had always done some type of devotional, but this was different. This was a love affair, and I craved time alone with Jesus and the Holy Spirit. It became more important than anything else in my life.

Take Him with You

I really enjoy a great chick flick, and many times God has used movies to speak to me. Once I was watching the movie *Stepmom*, when the Holy Spirit began to speak to my heart about my relationship with Him and with the Holy Spirit.

There is a scene at the end of the movie when the mom, Jackie, is near the end of her battle with cancer and knows she is going to die soon. On Christmas morning, Jackie meets with her two children individually to give them the special gifts she has made. They talk about her death and what it will be like when she is gone. First she talks with her son, Ben, and then her daughter, Anna. As she and Anna look at the quilt of memories Jackie has made for her, Anna begins to cry and tells her mom she is going to miss her so much when she is gone. Jackie then replies:

> It's okay to miss me. You can miss me and you can take me with you. You can. When you're in trouble, have me there. When you fall in love, have me there. You can. That's how people go on forever, you know, because someone takes them along. Your graduation, your wedding, and when you have your babies, take me along. Will you?[1]

As I watched this scene, I heard the Holy Spirit whisper that same line—"Take me with you." Then He went on, "You can take me with you every day. Make me a part of every single thing in your life from the moment you wake up." The Holy Spirit wanted to be with me as a best friend. I never had to do life alone, even in the simplicity of my daily activities, I could have His presence with me.

After this, I learned how to connect to His presence by acknowledging Him throughout my day. I would tell the Holy Spirit, "You really are the best friend a girl could have. You know me better than I know myself." I would fellowship with the Holy Spirit when I went grocery shopping, as I was cooking, going for a walk, doing laundry, everything. I became more aware of the Holy Spirit's voice, and I would get spiritual downloads or have encounters in the most random moments. The more this happened, the more I cherished it and looked forward to the next time it might happen.

God Wants to Talk to Me

God is always speaking, and He loves to speak to me in different ways. It is not only through the Word of God, but also through a good book, a movie, friends, ministers, family and a million other little ways.

Many people are all about the Word, the Word, the Word. Others are all about signs, dreams, visions and feeling God's presence. There is a little saying about this that goes: "If all you do is read the Word you will become puffed up (prideful) and if all you do is follow the spirit you will blow-up (get flakey)." I believe in having a relationship with the person of Jesus and not just the words on the page of my Bible. Many times the Holy Spirit would lead me to scripture that would confirm what I learned and received through our relationship.

> *You have your heads in your Bibles constantly because you think you'll find eternal life there. But you miss the forest for the trees. These Scriptures are all about me! And here I am, standing right before you, and you aren't willing to receive from me the life you say you want (John 5:39 MSG).*

Jesus still has so much He wants to tell us, and not just through the Bible. He is still speaking even now.

> *There is so much more I would like to say to you, but it's more than you can grasp at this moment. But when the truth-giving Spirit comes, he will unveil the reality of every truth within you. He won't speak on his own, but only what he hears from the Father, and he will reveal prophetically to you what is to come (John 16:12–13 TPT).*

For the last several years, the Holy Spirit has told me to name my year and then has given me exactly what to name it. I knew He would do it again this year, so several weeks before January I asked Him: "What do you want me to call this year?" When I didn't hear anything right away, I soon forgot all about it. On New Year's Eve, my husband took me to a fine dining restaurant to celebrate. As soon as I went to cut into my steak, I heard the Holy Spirit whisper, "Fulfillment. That's what I want you to name this year."

I was totally caught off guard. The word *fulfillment* had never even crossed my mind when I asked Him what to name it. I never would have come up with that on my own, but the minute He spoke it, I knew that was it. I had heard from heaven, and I felt the love of the Father and His smile of approval. At that moment, I felt His joy and had an instant sense of expectation. With this as the name of my year, what could the Father possibly have in mind? I felt excited and full of hope.

God has always desired to be to be intimately involved in every detail of our lives. I love when the Holy Spirit speaks and I'm not expecting it, or when He does something I know could not have happened without divine intervention. My life is a constant story of what I call *God winks*—those things that happen that are undeniably Him. Walking in intimacy and union is an incredible adventure. Many times He has spoken something that has altered the course of my life, or He has given me an extraordinary gift that I never would have expected.

Places and Spaces

God has spoken to me in different ways at different times in my life. I learned to be sensitive to where I felt the Holy Spirit drawing me to meet, whether it was at my home, the lakefront, or even walking in my neighborhood. Where I would go to get alone with Him would change on a regular basis.

Many mornings I felt the need to be outside, so I would go to the lakefront to spend time with Him. I would go sit at my little spot, look out over the water, and just let His presence soak into my being. I felt grateful for such a beautiful place to spend time with Him and enjoy the beauty of His creation. I relished that He had made all of this simply for His children to enjoy. I believe He has this for all of us, but He wants us to look for it.

My home is another thing I am deeply grateful for. As my kids have grown up and left the house, there are more and more places I can go to spend time alone with God. In the cooler, fall months, or on sunny, winter days, I love sitting in the sunroom at the back of the house. As the sun streams through the windows, I can look out at the beautiful foliage and enjoy the change in seasons from the comfort of my corner chair. In the cold, winter months, I spend a lot of time in a cozy, upstairs bedroom. I love to curl up in bed with my Bible in my lap and a cup of coffee on the table beside me.

I find pleasure in simply *being* with Jesus, and it is part of the adventure to see where He wants to meet with me throughout different seasons.

Protecting Connection

After my encounter in 2006, I continuously made hearing God's voice and staying connected to Him the most important thing in my life. This did not mean I was never distracted, but when I was, I could feel it. Because nothing compared to intimate connection, I learned to put Him first before everything else. I set aside extended periods of time just to read my Bible, pray, and soak in His presence.

I also began to guard my connection. When you really love someone, you protect your connection with them. No one wants to be in a relationship and feel as if you are just going through the motions. I don't want this with my earthly husband, and I don't want this with Jesus either. After experiencing habitation, I would never be satisfied with visitation. Can you imagine if your earthly husband only came to visit and did not live in your house with you? This scenario gives a bit of perspective about what Jesus wants with us when we marry Him.

In the past, to protect my relationship with Jesus, I had an outward focus of *Don't do this, and don't do that.* Protecting my relationship from the outside, although important, could not take care of the deep recesses of my heart. I found that if I took care of my heart, my heart would take care of everything else. My walk with Jesus became all about the inside job.

Just like I protected connection with my husband, I protected connection with the Lord. If I felt like something was off between us, I didn't ignore it, hoping it would just go away. I made a point to get to the bottom of what was wrong. I would ask the Holy Spirit if I had done anything to grieve or offend Him, and if I had, I would quickly ask for forgiveness. I watched over the tenderness and passion of my heart toward Jesus on a daily basis.

> *At each and every sunrise you will hear my voice as I prepare my sacrifice of prayer to you. Every morning I lay out the pieces of my life on the altar and wait for your fire to fall upon my heart (Psalms 5:3 TPT).*

When Things Get Rocky

The enemy will always seek to pull us away from intimate connection with the Lord. There have actually been many times when this has happened to me. Almost every time, it was because things didn't work out the way I thought, and my initial reaction was disappointment. During those times, I would have to continually remind myself of the truth so the lies of the enemy didn't take up residence in my heart. The enemy will always call the goodness of God into question, but because of my history with His goodness and my foundation in His Word, I was able to move past these times of disconnection quickly by meditating on the truth.

I can't live without connection anymore because it is something I have become accustomed to. Now when I feel disconnected, I lean in even closer and ask the Holy Spirit to search my heart for anything that might be amiss.

> *God, I invite your searching gaze into my heart. Examine me through and through; find out everything that may be hidden within me. Put me to the test and sift through all my anxious cares. See if there is any path of pain I'm walking on, and lead me back to your glorious, everlasting way—the path that brings me back to you (Psalms 139:23–24 TPT).*

Once the enemy knew that I would pursue connection and love at all costs, the battles (although intense) did not last as long. Once love became the driving force of my walk with God, the enemy lost his grip. My love would always outlast my self-discipline. During these seasons of testing, I learned to persevere, trust, and lean in closer rather than retreat.

> *Blessed [happy, spiritually prosperous, favored by God] is the man who is steadfast under trial and perseveres when tempted; for when he has passed the test and been approved, he will receive the [victor's] crown of life which the Lord has promised to those who love Him (James 1:12 AMP).*

Going through trials and difficulties is never fun, but it has always been worth it. On the other side of each test of my faith, there has been a reward. I have always experienced tremendous growth as a result of staying steadfast to Jesus in the midst of the trial. When I was finally on the other side, I could sense His approval, and that alone felt like enough, but the reward was always more of Him.

Habitation

My focus above every other pursuit was maintaining my connection and union with Jesus. I was no longer waiting for some special visitation like I had been in the past. I now understood that I could live in a place of constant habitation (dwelling with God in continual connection and no longer feeling separated). This is what I had been looking for all of my life. The veil that had hidden Jesus's face and true identity had been removed. I was experiencing constant face-to-face and heart-to-heart, and I knew I could never go back. Habitation became the foundation of my walk with God.

Chapter 9

The Word and His Words

Reading the Word after Christ had lifted the veil changed how I was perceiving things. I was reading the Word through a lens of love, and I could feel it revolutionizing me from the inside. I literally began to meditate day and night, just like David talks about in the book of Psalms. The Word of God had always been an important part of my life, but after marrying Jesus and coming into total union, it became not just a part of my life, but my very life.

> But Jesus replied, "It is written and forever remains written, 'Man shall not live by bread alone, but by every word that comes out of the mouth of God'" (Matthew 4:4 AMP).

Making Him my first love had opened the windows of heaven again, and I was encountering Jesus in His Word on a daily basis. During this time, it was just me, Jesus, the Holy Spirit, and the Word of God. I had pulled back from being involved in church for a season to be alone with God and to allow Him to do a deeper work in me. As I spent time in the Word, wrong mindsets I had about Him were being uprooted. I stopped feeling guilty about having to follow some kind of Bible reading plan, and I began to let the Holy Spirit lead me in what to read on a daily basis. I was totally undone by the revelation I was receiving in God's Word, and I could not get enough. As I read, I could feel the Word of God restoring my soul, and it was like being hooked up to a spiritual IV that put life back inside. I was eating from the tree of life, and it was better than anything I had ever tasted.

Hearing for Myself

The Father wanted me to walk in such intimate fellowship with Him that I didn't have to live my life through second hand revelation. It would never be enough to depend on someone else to feed me. Jesus wanted me to get into the Word of God to hear His voice for myself and be taught by the Holy Spirit.

> But you have received the Holy Spirit, and he lives within you, so you don't need anyone to teach you what is true. For the Spirit teaches you everything you need to know, and what he teaches is true—it is not a lie. So just as he has taught you, remain in fellowship with Christ (1 John 2:27 NLT).

My true spiritual growth came from soaking myself in the Word of God and spending a lot of time in His presence. The more time I spent with Him, the more familiar I became with His voice, and I learned more and more how to discern the inner promptings of the Holy Spirit. The Holy Spirit taught me that God had a frequency my spirit could actually sense. His voice brought peace to my heart, even in correction, and it always lined up with not only the Word, but also His character and nature.

I grew in my ability to hear God's voice for myself, and often what I heard being preached simply acted as a confirmation to what the Holy Spirit had already been teaching me. Don't get me wrong, I love fresh revelation brought by great teaching or preaching, but there is nothing more thrilling than having what the Lord has already taught you confirmed by a pastor or teacher you know and trust. Having the Holy Spirit confirm what I have already been taught, has given me confidence that I am hearing clearly for myself.

The Holy Spirit began to show me what God approved of through training me to discern what was excellent. Before this, my whole Christian life had been about discerning and avoiding evil rather than knowing what is good and pleasing to the Father. Think about people who are trained to spot fake money. They don't train these people by having them handle fake bills. They give them real bills over and over and over so that when a fake bill comes across their path, they immediately know it's a fake. I think that's how God wants us to be. He wants us to become so familiar with Him, His ways, His voice, and the truth, that when something is off and not of Him, we know it immediately.

> *But solid food is for the mature, whose spiritual senses perceive heavenly matters. And they have been adequately trained by what they've experienced to emerge with understanding of the difference between what is truly excellent and what is evil and harmful (Hebrews 5:14 TPT).*

Will I Be Deceived?

As a believer, I was taught to obey all spiritual authority so that I remained under God's covering. As a result, I developed an unhealthy fear around obeying authority, but not all authority is correct or good. This is why it is so important to be led by the Holy Spirit—so we can discern what is from God and what is not. The unsound teaching I received had taught me not to trust my own heart, because if I did, I might somehow be deceived. For years I was naive, and I allowed fear to rule in this area. It was one of my greatest battles. One day, when I was really struggling with the fear of being deceived, the Holy Spirit began to quote the following verse to me.

> *"You parents—if your children ask for a loaf of bread, do you give them a stone instead? Or if they ask for a fish, do you give them a snake? Of course not!" (Matthew 7:9–10 NLT)*

I was asking and seeking for truth, and I was reading my Bible consistently, so why would He allow me to be led into deception? Jesus comforted me with His Word and assured me that I could trust Him to keep me on the right path as I followed His voice.

> *When he has brought out all his own, he goes on ahead of them, and his sheep follow him because they know his voice (John 10:4 NIV).*

After this moment, I began to trust the Spirit of God within me. He showed me that His laws had been written on my heart, so I did not need to worry that my own heart might deceive me.

"For this is the covenant that I will make with the house of Israel after those days, says the Lord: I will put My laws in their mind and write them on their hearts; and I will be their God, and they shall be My people. None of them shall teach his neighbor, and none his brother, saying, 'Know the Lord,' for all shall know Me, from the least of them to the greatest of them" (Hebrews 8:10–11 NKJV).

One of the best things my mom ever taught me was to "never doubt in the dark what God has spoken to you in the light." I don't know how many times I have gone back to this one simple statement and asked myself: *What did you hear in your heart when you knew you couldn't deny it was God?*

Rhema Words

I had spent a lifetime in the Word, but I had not always spiritually discerned it; therefore, it had no power to truly change me. Knowing the Word in my head would never make it real to my heart unless I was able to receive revelation from the Holy Spirit. Without the Holy Spirit's breath on the words, they were just that—words. With the Holy Spirit's breath, they became spirit and life.

I had gotten revelation from God's Word in many different seasons of my life, but there were also times I felt like I was just reading to be reading and checking off a box. If you asked me later in the day what I had read that morning, most of the time I probably couldn't tell you. Now when I read the Word, it was jumping off the pages right into my heart. I was receiving deep revelation from God on a regular basis, and there was nothing boring about it. This has continued in my life for over fifteen years. It has been consistently alive, and I have never gone back to reading just to be reading.

> It is the Spirit who gives life; the flesh conveys no benefit [it is of no account]. The **words** I have spoken to you are spirit and life [providing eternal life] (John 6:63 AMP, emphasis added).

In this particular verse, "words" is the Greek word *rhemas*.[1] A rhema is when God breathes on His Logos (the written word), and it becomes a word of life just for you. No longer is it just words on a page, but the Spirit of God delivers those words straight into your heart.

This is how we were intended to live. The Word of God is much more than a Bible, it is a person. Jesus was the Word made manifest. As I spent time in the Word of God, I encountered Jesus there, and I knew they were His words spoken directly to me.

> You search the Scriptures, for in them you think you have eternal life; and these are they which testify of Me. But you are not willing to come to Me that you may have life (John 5:39–40 NKJV).

God breathed rhema began to totally transform my life. The Word of God was ministering to my heart, and it was not only changing the way I thought, but also how I perceived God, life, myself, and even those around me. The Holy Spirit always knew exactly what I needed to hear and when I needed to hear it. On a regular basis, He would bring a verse to mind. Sometimes I didn't know the whole verse or its location, but I could pull out my phone and easily find it. Thank goodness for the gift of technology! Those verses were spirit and life in those moments.

The Holy Spirit will teach us if we have ears to hear what the Spirit of the Lord is saying. We don't have to be a minister or have a degree in Theology. I was just a simple woman with nothing other than a heart to hear.

The Power of a Decree

I was aware of making a decree, but it wasn't until the Holy Spirit led me to this one particular verse in Job that I began to understand the *full power* of a decree.

> *If you lay gold in the dust . . . And make the Almighty your gold and [the Lord] your precious silver treasure, Then you will have delight in the Almighty, and you will lift up your face to God. You will make your prayer to Him, and He will hear you . . . You shall also decide and decree a thing, and it shall be established for you; and the light [of God's favor] shall shine upon your ways (Job 22:24–28 AMPC).*

I don't believe this verse is for the casual believer. There was a time when I would have been lying to myself if I thought the Lord was my precious treasure. Yes, I was in church every time the doors opened. I prayed and read my Bible, but He was not my most precious treasure.

When God became my most precious treasure, I laid down the things that got in the way of my time with Him. I made Him the first priority of my life. He was on my mind all of the time, just like when I fell in love with my husband. I knew with all of my heart that I had laid my gold in the dust, and He was the most valuable thing I had. The end of this verse gave me the confidence to know that I could decree a thing and see it established. I went to the throne room armed with the Word of God.

This next verse in Job became another scripture I had in my arsenal of weapons against the enemy. I knew I could go to God on behalf of someone else, based on my own walk with Him, and expect to see answers to my prayers, and I did.

> *He will even deliver one who is not innocent; Yes, he will be delivered by the purity of your hands (Job 22:30 NKJV).*

What a powerful verse! This verse has been such a blessing to my heart when I have been praying for others in tough situations. No matter where they were at in their relationship with God, I was able to stand in the gap and believe for their deliverance. This is an awesome verse for mama's with children away from God. Another verse I love to decree is:

> *The wicked shall not be unpunished: but the seed of the righteous shall be delivered (Proverbs 11:21 KJV).*

In faith, I have declared this over and over for my children and have seen it come to pass.

Chapter 10

Becoming a Believing Believer

I had been a believer since I was fourteen years old, but at forty-six, the Holy Spirit revealed to me that although I called myself a believer, in most areas of my life, fear still ruled. I was not a believing believer at all, and unfortunately up until that point, I hadn't even been aware.

Changing My Belief System

The power of belief is a principal in God's Word whether we know Jesus as Lord or not. We really do receive what we actually believe, not what we think we believe. If we believe bad things will happen, they usually do, and God's Word confirms this.

> *For the thing which I greatly fear comes upon me, and that of which I am afraid befalls me (Job 3:25 AMP).*

The Holy Spirit opened my eyes to how much fear I still walked in, and how it had dictated my life. When I recognized how I had been so affected by fear, I made a commitment in my heart to become a believing believer. I asked the Holy Spirit to rip out every lie I believed about God, about myself, and others. I wanted to be able to stake my life on the Word of God and not on my experience, and this is exactly what began to happen.

After I came to the bitter end of myself and encountered His love, my eyes were opened. I began to understand His true nature and character. The Holy Spirit led me to verse after verse of scripture about His goodness and kindness and unconditional love for me. Even though I had read these verses in the past, it was as if I was reading them for the first time. His perfect love began to confront the fear I had buried deep inside my heart.

> *Love never brings fear, for fear is always related to punishment. But love's perfection drives the fear of punishment far from our hearts. Whoever walks constantly afraid of punishment has not reached love's perfection (1 John 4:18 TPT).*

Defeating every lie that called God's goodness into question was the most important part of my becoming a believing believer. How could I ever be a believing believer if there was even one shred of doubt about God's goodness? Any unbelief or doubt of His absolute goodness and kindness had to be completely uprooted.

True Nature and Character

When my eyes were opened to His goodness, and the lie that He might be holding out on me was destroyed, I was able to focus on

His nature rather than be overwhelmed by the circumstances of life. In every negative situation, I pressed into my understanding of His goodness and kindness rather than my circumstances. I knew I could trust Him because of who He was, and I camped out on this truth alone. When I felt unsure about life, the world, and the situations around me, the one thing I was certain of was His goodness.

God continued to transform the way I saw Him. The more I felt His love and experienced His goodness, the more I was able to trust Him. The connection between love and trust became so clear. One day I was thinking about this when He spoke to my heart and said, "The reason many people have a hard time trusting me is because they don't really have a true revelation of my love for them." I knew this was true because this is exactly what I had felt, but when I experienced His love firsthand, it changed everything.

When I was first born again, I knew Jesus loved me unconditionally, but after years of struggling with sin, I believed He was disappointed in me. I bought into a very religious view of the Lord and started to see Him as a hard task master who was hard to please. One day, when I was reading the parable of the talents, my eyes were opened to the deeper meaning, and I was able to see just how wrong this viewpoint had been.

> *"Then the one who had been entrusted with one thousand gold coins came to his master and said, 'Look, sir. I know that you are a hard man to please and you're a shrewd and ruthless businessman who grows rich on the backs of others. I was afraid of you, so I went and hid your money and buried it in the ground. But here it is—take it, it's yours.' But his master said to him, 'You're an untrustworthy and lazy servant! If you knew I was a shrewd and ruthless business man who always makes a profit, why*

*didn't you deposit my money in the bank?'" (Matthew
25:24–26 TPT)*

In the past, I had wondered why the master was so angry with the
servant for what he did with his talent. When I read it again, I saw
something I never had before, and suddenly, I understood. The
servant *did* hide his talent, but the *reason* he did was because of what
he believed about the master.

In this parable, the master represents God, and we are the servant.
Because the servant didn't know the master's true heart or intentions,
he misjudged him and accused him of being something he wasn't.
This is what upset the master. As this revelation sank in, it broke my
heart. It was a moment of true repentance for me. My eyes had been
veiled by a spirit of religion, and my perception of who God was had
become very cloudy. Now the Holy Spirit was revealing His true
heart to me again.

One revelation after another, my heart was being changed. God was
not a hard task master, and He did not need me to be a workhorse. In
fact, the greatest thing I would ever do for God was believe Him.

> *Then they asked Him, "What are we to do, so that we may habitu-
> ally be doing the works of God?" Jesus answered, "This is the
> work of God: that you believe [adhere to, trust in, rely on, and
> have faith] in the One whom He has sent" (John 6:28–29 AMP).*

When I read this verse in the Amplified Bible, it reverberated
through my spirit like never before. I had read this many times, but I
had never registered what it was actually saying until I read it in the
Amplified with revelation from the Holy Spirit. The WORK He
wanted me to do was BELIEVE!

What I did not realize at the time, was just how much work this would actually be.

A Hard Truth

> *Know and understand that it is [really] the people [who live] by faith who are [the true] sons of Abraham (Galatians 3:7 AMP).*

Now the Holy Spirit really had my attention. Honestly, I had read this scripture more times than I could count, and I even knew it by heart. As I began to meditate on this verse, I realized what I believe about God is a really big deal, so much so that God called Abraham righteous because of his faith. Not because of what he was doing, but because of what he believed (Gen. 15:6). I began to ask myself if I had lived as a true son of Abraham, and I realized I hadn't.

Seeing myself as someone who had walked in great faith, and then realizing I hadn't, really affected me. I came to a place of deep repentance in this area of my life. You can think you've walked in faith all of your life, and then in one day, the Holy Spirit can pull back the curtain and show you every area where this was not the case. Even when things were not working out the way I anticipated, what God wanted was faith that trusted in His goodness and loving kindness.

Trusting God with My Children

It has been some years now, but at one point I was carrying so many burdens for my adult children that I was actually having symptoms of a heart attack—chest pains, shortness of breath, exhaustion, and so forth. I ended up in the cardiologist office. The first thing he asked me was if I had any anxiety. "Yes, I have anxiety. I have five adult children!" What I didn't know back then was that stress could mimic a heart attack. After they ran some tests and found nothing wrong with me physically, I knew I had a different type of heart problem.

One day after this happened, I was on the lakefront spending time with God. I opened the *Jesus Calling* devotional on my phone, and the first line read, "Entrust your loved ones to me; release them to my protective care. They are much safer with me than your clinging hands."[1] Then I heard the Holy Spirit speak straight to my heart: "You are carrying a burden I have already carried for you. Don't you know I love your kids even more than you do?" I knew He was right. I was literally allowing myself to be crushed under a load I was never intended to carry. Jesus showed me clearly that He had already sacrificed Himself for everything they would ever need, and I could trust Him because as much as I loved my children, He loved them even more. That day on the lakefront marked the beginning of me being able to release my children into God's hands.

I started to recognize that most of my life I had coddled fear, and I had not been able to see it as a sin. Right then and there, I acknowledged my fear to God and asked for forgiveness. I was able to see how having fear was literally inviting the enemy to work and having faith actually invited God to work. My fear and unbelief had limited the work of God not only in my life, but also in the lives of my family. Now I understood why fear and unbelief were so offensive to Jesus.

The Sin of Unbelief

One of my biggest challenges in becoming a believing believer was listening to God's voice and believing what He said over the reasonings of my mind. When the Holy Spirit gave me a rhema for my life, my husband, or my children, I would plant it in the garden of my heart. How I stewarded and tended that word would determine if the seed ever produced fruit. When things got hard, I could fall back into logic and abort the promise before it had a chance to come forth, or I could keep watering the seed He had given me and see the fruit of prayers answered and promises fulfilled. My act of obedience was to water the seed and keep the weeds of unbelief out of the garden of my heart.

> *"The seed that fell into good, fertile soil represents those lovers of truth who hear it deep within their hearts. They respond by clinging to the word, keeping it dear as they endure all things in faith. This is the seed that will one day bear much fruit in their lives" (Luke 8:15 TPT).*

It was very clear to me that becoming a believing believer was paramount if I wanted to see God's will fulfilled in my life and in my family. Every time something came up, whether it was with my children, my marriage, or other circumstances, I learned to go to God with it. This took discipline on my part, especially when I wanted to reach out to others for advice or opinions. Instead I learned to dialogue with God, leaning in, getting quiet, and listening for His counsel.

In the midst of trials, we have a choice—we can either choose to believe the voice of God or believe the voice of fear. One day I was struggling with who I would believe when the Holy Spirit spoke to me and said, "You know, fear has a voice. When fear calls, you don't have to answer."

Can You Worship?

Many times in the heat of the battle, I would hear the Holy Spirit whisper, "Exalt me over the situation. Make me higher than the problem. Exalt me, not the problem." Worship became my every breath during my most difficult trials. I remember waking up one night in sheer panic and torment over something going on in my family. The Lord spoke clearly to my heart that He wanted me to worship and just focus on His goodness. I knew in my spirit, if everything fell apart and things went to hell in a hand basket, I still needed to remain in an attitude of worship.

Real worship is not just when things are hunky dory. It's when life literally feels like it's falling apart, and you choose Him. You choose to exalt Him and camp out on His goodness. It's when you say: "I may not understand, and I hurt like hell right now, but I love you, and I know you are good. You are faithful, and I will be a believing believer. I choose to trust you. I choose surrender."

> Then I will say to my soul, "Don't be discouraged; don't be disturbed, for I fully expect my Savior-God to break through for me. Then I'll have plenty of reasons to praise him all over again." Yes, he is my saving grace! (Psalms 43:5 TPT)

Worship became my warfare. It became the way I fought my battles. Every time a situation came up that was out of my control, I pressed in even more. I broke open my alabaster box at the feet of Jesus.

This is how I was able to keep from completely falling apart. The Holy Spirit has used gratitude and worship to pull my heart out of despair and bring me back to the secret place so many times. Whenever I focus on His goodness, I can get unstuck. This has been such a gift to me in so many seasons.

A Lesson from Job

The question that resounded when life felt like it was crumbling around me was *What do I really believe, and will I trust Him?*

> *Though he slay me, yet will I trust in him: but I will maintain mine own ways before him (Job 13:15 KJV).*

Before God removed His hedge of protection from Job, Job only knew God in a very peripheral way. Then, in the midst of his heartache, God revealed Himself to Job and showed him His heart. After all that Job walked through, he came to admit:

> *"I have heard of You by the hearing of the ear, But now my eye sees You. Therefore I abhor myself, And repent in dust and ashes" (Job 42:5–6 NKJV).*

I believe that through His trial, Job recognized His own heart and truly repented. Our heart and what we really believe is often revealed through our deepest trials. I know mine was. This was when my true beliefs about God and the things He had spoken to me went through the refiner's fire. What I really believed had to be tried and tested to come forth as gold.

Now that I had a new lens, I could see that even when bad things had happened in my life, Jesus had never quit pursuing me with His love and His goodness. I saw that living in this broken world, I could expect tribulation and loss. None of us get to choose our pain. If I dumped out all of my heartaches along with my other brothers and sisters in Christ, I would probably choose to take mine back rather than someone else's. I can truly say my greatest heartaches have brought me closer to God. I call them a *sweet hurt*. I would not have chosen them for myself, but because I have walked <u>through</u> them, I am grateful.

And we know [with great confidence] that God [who is deeply concerned about us] causes all things to work together [as a plan] for good for those who love God, to those who are called according to His plan and purpose (Romans 8:28 AMP).

Chapter 11

Tending the Garden of Your Heart

And I will give you a new heart, and I will put a new spirit in you. I will take out your stony, stubborn heart and give you a tender, responsive heart (Ezekiel 36:26 NLT).

Through my union with Jesus, I learned how to walk with Him in the garden of my heart. God has given me the great privilege of stewarding my heart, and His desire is for this to become one of the most natural parts of my life. I get to choose what I plant, what I water, and what I allow to grow in my garden.

Fertile Soil

Nothing feels worse to me than having a hard heart. That's why I pay attention to it more than anything. The most valuable thing in my walk with God is having a tender, faith-filled, believing heart.

Guard your heart above all else, for it determines the course of your life (Proverbs 4:23 NLT).

When I feel myself moving away from being tender-hearted, red flags start popping up inside. This is the fear of the Lord in my life, and it's the good kind of fear, because what I actually fear is disconnection from Him. If I ever get to the place in my walk with God, or even in my earthly marriage, where I feel like I am just going through the motions, there is something going on in my heart that needs to be addressed. Discerning my heart is like taking my spiritual temperature.

One of the biggest things that causes hardness of heart for me is disappointment. Because this has tripped me up in the past, I have made a point to stay aware of it. When I feel disappointed, I specifically choose to think of all the good things God has done in my life to help me keep my heart soft. Another thing that trips me up is going into self-protection mode. Even when it's really painful, I choose to stay vulnerable and let God be my defense and the protector of my heart. This can be so hard sometimes, but when I choose vulnerability, and I don't harden or fight back, His grace always comes.

Ungratefulness

After I married the Lord and came into union, one of the first things the Holy Spirit began to deal with was how I saw my life. My tendency was to focus on what was wrong rather than what was right. I never realized how much time and energy had been directed on what I felt was missing. When Jesus lifted my veil after our union, I was able to see clearly all that I had to be thankful for. My eyes were opened to the truth about myself, and when I saw how ungrateful I had been, it broke my heart. I was sad I had spent so much of my life not having God's perspective.

After my eyes were opened, the Holy Spirit lovingly showed me what I looked like by painting a picture in my mind. First, I saw a grateful child who was delighted with every single thing you did for them, and then I saw another child, who no matter what you did, it was never enough. Then the Holy Spirit asked me a question: "Which one would you want to bless?"

This revelation changed me, and there was a shift in my heart from that moment on. No longer did I compare my life to other people. I was content with the life Jesus had given me, and I became a true worshiper on the inside. My worship wasn't just an act I did on Sunday morning, but it became the posture of my heart toward God on a day-to-day and moment-by-moment basis.

Gratitude became a key to unlock doors of my heart that had been shut from the light of God's presence. I became very sensitive to anything that shifted me out of the posture of gratitude. Being thankful brought me right into His presence, and it became one of the greatest keys to my closeness with the Lord.

Pride

One particular time, my heart felt so anxious that I could not feel the Lord's closeness like I usually did. I really had no idea what was wrong, but I desperately wanted revelation so I could get to the bottom of it. I reached out to a friend who does inner healing, but before we could ever meet, the Holy Spirit met me on my own.

I was at a women's ministry meeting, and during worship, the Holy Spirit gave me a vision. In the vision, I was wearing a shiny vest that looked like it was made from some kind of metal. I was sporting the vest like "Hey, look at me. Aren't I something?" I knew what I saw in my vision had meaning, but at that time, I had no idea what it was.

The next day I went to the lakefront to pray and process. I asked the Holy Spirit, "What in the world did that vision of me wearing the vest mean?" I knew He had given me the vision to help me get unstuck. I heard the Holy Spirit tell me that the vest represented unnecessary burdens I was carrying, and I had thought they looked good on me. Then I heard the word "pride," and it all started to unravel.

Jesus showed me that I had carried unnecessary burdens for my children because I thought it was the more nurturing thing to do. Then He showed me how carrying those burdens made me feel like I was a better mother, but it was all rooted in pride. Not really a pretty picture. Carrying things God never intended for me to carry didn't make me a better mother; it made me an unhealthy one, in body, soul and spirit.

I asked God to forgive me for my pride. As soon as I did, I saw a vision of God removing the shiny, heavy vest, and I immediately felt a huge weight lift off. This was something I had carried for a very long time. Both pride and anxiety had been affecting my heart, and I had not even been aware of it. The Holy Spirit wanted to get my attention by bringing the issue right to the surface, knowing that I was ready to look at this area of my life and deal with it. I was able to get freedom when I agreed with God and repented for both my pride and my fear. I could trust Him to take care of my children. I would continue to pray for them, but I would no longer carry something He never designed for me to carry.

Judging Others and Yourself

Besides pride making us think we can carry things that are way too big, it can also make us think we are smart enough to be the judge— of ourselves and others. Most of my Christian life, I viewed myself through the lens of self-judgment. Living with self-judgment actually felt very normal. I could never be too hard on myself, and somewhere along the way, I came to believe that this was a good thing. I think it just made me feel better, but unfortunately this was probably rooted in pride as well.

Because I wanted to be completely whole in every area of my life, I gave the Holy Spirit permission to show me anything I needed to deal with. One area was all of the judgments I had made about myself. He spoke to me and said, "It's time to let go of all your self-judgment. It's not serving you well." I remember getting on my face to pray, and I saw that once again, this was rooted in pride. I acknowledged my pride and self-judgment to the Father, and I asked Him to forgive me. Right after I prayed, I heard the Holy Spirit say, "It's time to let yourself off the hook." I looked inside of my heart and saw all of the ways I had judged myself, and I just let it all go. I immediately felt lighter, and I breathed in His sweetness.

After this powerful time with the Holy Spirit, I not only let myself off the hook, but I started to let others off the hook as well. I began to see that many times when I had judged someone for something, I ended up doing the very same thing. One time I had judged this family, thinking they were so ridiculously religious. Well, guess what happened? About five years later, we became just like them. We were super religious, following all of these strict outward standards and thinking we were better than others because of it. Another time I remember judging someone who had gotten hurt and offended in church. I remember thinking *How ridiculous? I've never been hurt in church. How is that possible?* Well, a few years after this, I experienced hurt after hurt because of some major moral failures from leadership. I thought about what I said in my heart about the person who got hurt, and I realized I had set myself up by my own judgment.

> *No matter who you are, before you judge the wickedness of others, you had better remember this: you are also without excuse, for you too are guilty of the same kind of things! When you judge others, and then do the same things they do, you condemn yourself (Romans 2:1 TPT).*

The footnotes for this verse in the passion translation explain:

> The Aramaic can be translated "Because of this, O human, the Spirit is not speaking through you as you judge another, **for against what you judge, you will also revert.**"

Maybe this is where the saying "What you judge, you become" came from. From that moment on, I made a decision to stay humble and let God do the judging, knowing I could be in the same boat if I wasn't careful. If I found myself doing it, I would quickly ask God to forgive me, cleanse me, and take back any ground I had given the enemy by my own judgment.

For you'll be judged by the same standard that you've used to judge others. The measurement you use on them will be used on you (Matthew 7:2 TPT).

Many times life experience proves to be the best teacher. This was definitely true for me. I have come to see that we really do reap what we sow. With that in mind, I started to sow more and more grace and less and less judgment.

Unforgiveness, Bitterness, and Offense

Many times I felt challenged with feelings of unforgiveness that I just couldn't get rid of. One of the hardest times was when I had to forgive someone who had not done something to me personally, but to someone I loved. For me, this is usually the most difficult type of offense to forgive, and it requires even more grace.

Day after day, I went to the lakefront to process with the Lord over what this person had done. I poured out my heart to Him. We talked back and forth about the offense that had been committed. I knew Jesus had forgiven me over and over, so I needed to forgive this person too, but my heart just felt so broken and so angry that it seemed impossible. This went on for months.

My life felt dark during this battle, but even in this hard place, I felt God's love for me. I knew I had to fight for forgiveness. I could not allow it to pull me into a bottomless pit and destroy me from the inside. As wrong as I thought this person was, I knew I had to forgive.

After months of yielding my heart and choosing forgiveness over and over again, my heart was finally able to let go. I felt as if I had been given a divine gift. In many ways, my heart had been under temporary lockdown until I was able to forgive. Unforgiveness truly is such a hard taskmaster, and I am sure this is why the Word of God equates it to being in prison.

> *"And in wrath his master turned him over to the torturers (jailers) until he paid all that he owed. My heavenly Father will also do the same to [every one of] you, if each of you does not forgive his brother from your heart"* (Matthew 18:34–35 AMP).

After I forgave this person, forgiveness became less painful and not nearly as long and drawn out. I found that sometimes all I needed to let go and forgive was to get God's perspective and see the offender from His heart. This made all of the difference in the world. One time the Holy Spirit actually told me that I needed to let go of my right to an apology. I let go and asked Jesus to forgive me for my heart attitude, and the feeling of being offended left immediately.

Nothing feels worse than holding onto unforgiveness, even for a moment. The misery I felt when I could not forgive should have been enough, but my main motivation to forgive was actually my desire to have a pure heart and be able to hear God's voice clearly. This kept me plowing through opportunities to hold on to unforgiveness. Unforgiveness made me feel like I was in a fog that dimmed the light of God's presence, and this was a punishment in itself.

I know I've truly forgiven when after I have made the choice to forgive, my feelings ultimately follow. Choosing to forgive is an important part of the process, but if I don't feel it in my emotions, I know God has not finished the work on the inside of me. Most of my life I was taught to ignore my feelings, but feelings are actually a good indication of where the heart is. Just like I want to feel my love for God, I want to feel forgiveness.

> *Get rid of all bitterness, rage, anger, harsh words, and slander, as well as all types of evil behavior. Instead, be kind to each other, tenderhearted, forgiving one another, just as God through Christ has forgiven you (Ephesians 4:31–32 NLT).*

Bitterness, offense, and unforgiveness—whatever you choose to name what you're carrying inside—they all have the same ability to infect your heart with deadly poison. These are the things I have found to be the most harmful to my connection with God.

I think true forgiveness requires total humility and dependence on the power of Jesus, because I have absolutely no ability to do this in my own strength. When I was really struggling to forgive someone, it required yielding my heart to God in surrender over and over, asking Him to do what I could not do for myself. I could make the choice to forgive, but ultimately it was God who granted true forgiveness to my heart.

Forgiveness is an ongoing process in life. Almost every day we are presented with opportunities to hold onto things, or to let them go. Not everything will be huge; it may be something petty, but even hanging on to small irritations can affect the garden of your heart. Forgiveness has to become a lifestyle if we want to live in a place of freedom and clear connection with Jesus.

Chapter 12

Becoming a Child Again

As I continued to see Jesus through a lens of love rather than law, the Holy Spirit brought me back to several verses in the book of Mathew. When I began to read and meditate, I saw things about the kingdom of heaven that I had never seen before.

> *At that time the disciples came to Jesus and asked, "Who is greatest in the kingdom of heaven?" He called a little child and set him before them, and said, "I assure you and most solemnly say to you, unless you repent [that is, change your inner self—your old way of thinking, live changed lives] and become like children [trusting, humble, and forgiving], you will never enter the kingdom of heaven. Therefore, whoever humbles himself like this child is greatest in the kingdom of heaven" (Mathew 18:1–4 AMP).*

When I read these verses in the past, my eyes were veiled, but now that the veil had been lifted, I began to see them in relation to living in the kingdom realm. The kingdom of heaven was not just a destination, but a realm Jesus was inviting me to live in here on earth. The only way I was going to be able to enter this realm, was to become like a child.

Trusting

The very first quality Jesus was looking for was my childlike trust. For me to have faith and trust someone, I had to know they loved me. Now that I had experienced this radical, tangible love, I was able to really trust Jesus, for the first time. Before this, I was always trying to fix things myself rather than trusting Jesus to take care of it. Now I began to look to Him in total dependence, just like a child would look to their parents to take care of them. The problem was, I was so good at taking care of myself, I hardly knew how to let someone else do it, or even where to begin.

I decided to start by fully letting go of the real estate career I had put on pause. In my heart, I knew the only reason I had driven myself to get my license was because I did not trust God to take care of me. Although I knew letting it go was the right decision, it was still a struggle. I invested a lot of time and money, and I worked really hard to get my license. On top of that, I was really concerned with what other people would think of me if I just walked away. In my head I could just hear them saying, *What a waste.* But still, I knew this was what God wanted for me, and I needed to be obedient. Thankfully, my husband never gave me the slightest sense of disapproval. All he wanted was for me to obey God, and that took a lot of the pressure off. I walked away and went back to doing my baking business, which I enjoyed, but I would never make as much money baking as I could have with real estate.

What mattered more than money, was my childlike trust in God's ability to take care of our family. When I walked away in obedience and began to trust God, He blessed my husband more and more through his job. Our family was under God's divine order. There was a grace in my husband's life to provide for us that had not been there for me.

Before my encounter with love, I had always been very driven in my heart when it came to financial provision. This started as a result of feeling like if I wanted something, I had to get it for myself because no one else was going to. I started to believe my self-reliance was a good thing, and in some ways, it even felt honorable. This is why in the past, when there had not been any extra money in our budget for me, I started a baking business. I started this business just to have some spending money, but as time went on, I started taking on more and more household expenses. Then, if I wanted anything for myself, I just worked harder and longer. I had no idea how to let go and trust God and my husband. In my heart, I did not feel seen when it came to what I wanted. This changed as I began to trust. God blessed my surrender to Him in this area of my life. I never lacked for anything, and He miraculously met my heart's desires as I sought the kingdom first. I seemed to always find things at crazy deals, and I never had to strive. I just let the Holy Spirit lead me, and I always had more than enough.

Humble

Children are always growing and learning new things, but as an adult, it's easy to think we know it all. Sometimes even what we do know is wrong, and this is so often true in our relationship with God. In my journey of becoming childlike, Jesus invited me into a place of humility so I could relearn much of what I thought I knew about Him. Not only about Him, but also about what it meant to walk in the kingdom, and everything I thought I knew about Christianity. I had to become childlike and teachable. Pride would keep me stuck in old mindsets. Childlike humility would keep me growing, developing, and changing. It would require humility to see where I had been wrong about so many things in my life. This is one of those life lessons that never stops. Just when I think I know something, or I have arrived in an area, I find out I haven't.

Being childlike and humble meant becoming quick to allow the Holy Spirit to show me where I was wrong, no matter what area it applied to. Being prideful became a big stumbling block in our family when we homeschooled our children. Our standards, that we thought were so pure, separated us from other people and made us believe we were more holy. Pride convinced us we were right, but we had been totally wrong because God looks at the heart.

I also had to let go of my pride in order to see things from another person's perspective. This was especially true when it came to my children. I needed to be able to listen to their hearts and accept responsibility for the ways I had been wrong or had hurt them. Unfortunately, the saying "Mama knows best" is not always true. I had to choose to humble myself over and over again to give my kids a safe place to bring their grievances.

Another way I learned to walk in humility was asking God for his help instead of looking to my own strength. I learned from past experience that relying on my own ability was the path to failure. Living dependent on God is a mark of humility that I now gladly embrace. I carried the burden of independence and trying to make things happen on my own for way too long. Once I let go of my old way of living, I had no desire to go back.

My pursuit of wholeness and freedom was another area that I learned humility. I had to choose to let go of my old mindset of striving to be holy and righteous and just allow myself to be loved in the process. In the beginning, this felt totally wrong, but as I let go of what I thought was the right way to overcome sin and chose to accept God's opinion over mine, I received His grace and walked free.

> But He gives us more and more grace (power of the Holy Spirit, to meet this evil tendency and all others fully). That is why He says, God sets Himself against the proud and haughty, but gives grace [continually] to the lowly (those who are humble enough to receive it) (James 4:6 AMPC).

Letting go of my pride and humbly believing God, led me to the greatest breakthrough of my life. As you have already read about, I walked out of an eating disorder that I struggled with for over thirty years. I humbled myself when I realized what I had been trying all of those years, just wasn't working. The Holy Spirit showed me there was another way rather than what I had been taught my whole life, but I had to let go of control. I had to be childlike and trust Him. As I surrendered to love, I received the revelation I needed to walk completely free.

Forgiving

Children forgive so easily, especially when they are really young. One moment they can be mad at you and the next they are running into your arms, telling you that they love you. They don't hold onto things because they express their emotions immediately and without fear. This enables them to get the emotions out and be comforted in their pain. But what do we do as adults when we've been taught to control our emotions and not show them?

Growing up I was overwhelmed by my emotions, and as I got older, I became afraid of them. One emotion I really didn't know how to deal with was anger. Because I believed it was wrong to be angry, I buried it. I also buried a lot of other emotions, without even realizing it. All that did was give everything the perfect opportunity to fester and grow. When it came down to it, I was afraid of my feelings because I believed they defined me. Certain emotions I was okay with processing, but there were others I didn't want to identify with because of what I thought they said about me. Then one day, the Holy Spirit spoke to me and said, "Feelings are just feelings. They don't define you. It's what you do with them that matters."

Go ahead and be angry. You do well to be angry—but don't use your anger as fuel for revenge. And don't stay angry. Don't go to bed angry. Don't give the Devil that kind of foothold in your life (Ephesians 4:26–27 MSG).

Releasing my feelings in a healthy way, before they became deep rooted seeds that turned into resentment or bitterness, was key. My unresolved feelings had to be expressed. It was okay to feel them. That was the first step. I owned them, and then I talked to God about them just like I would a friend. I would process with the Lord until I was okay again. Sometimes I had to just talk and talk and talk. I think the Lord loves it when we talk to Him about what's in our hearts, just like a little child would.

Experiencing the Kingdom

Everything in me longed to experience more of God's kingdom realm. I used to believe the kingdom was about going to heaven, but Jesus tells us to pray, "Your kingdom come, your will be done, on earth as it is in heaven" (Matt. 6:10 ESV). Why would He want me to pray this way if it wasn't possible to experience His kingdom realm here? The more I thought about this, the more scriptures I had read all of my life began to explode on the inside of me. Scriptures like this one:

> *For the kingdom of God is not meat and drink; but righteousness, and peace, and joy in the Holy Ghost (Romans 14:17 KJV).*

This verse tells us that the kingdom is about the simplicity of doing what is right, being filled with peace, and living in a place of pure, childlike, joy! Once I was able to understand what it truly meant to live in the kingdom, I stopped trying to live according to a bunch of self-imposed rules and regulations. I actually started to enjoy my life, and I returned to being childlike. When I looked into the eyes of Jesus, I saw that He was so pleased with me. It was just like it was when I first got saved. When I first gave my life to Jesus, I would always have visions of Him swinging me around as a little girl. It was wonderful. And now for the first time, in a very long time, I believed it was okay to be a child once again.

Chapter 13

Heart Made Whole

One day, when I was on my face praying in my closet, I saw a vision of the Lord holding a heart in His hands. When I looked closer, I could see that He was not only holding it, but He was massaging it as well. As I stayed in this place of connection, I knew that this was not only my heart, but also the heart of many of His children. He spoke directly to my spirit that these hearts had stopped beating because of the traumas and disappointments they had been through. Then He told me, "I will take these hearts into my hands, and I will massage them with my love. And when I do, they will begin to beat again."

Not long after this vision, I ran into one of my doctor acquaintances at the hospital, just as he was coming out of surgery. It was a brief encounter, but I was able to ask him, "Is there ever a time in surgery when you have to go in and massage the heart to get it to beat again?" Without hesitation, he answered me and said, "The only time this happens is when there has been a trauma." When he said this, my whole body shook. I could hardly believe what I had just heard. I was blown away by his answer, and I knew what I had seen was from God. The Lord was telling me through my vision that He Himself would come and massage the broken, traumatized hearts of many believers and cause them to beat for Him again.

When God shows us something, we often think it is going to happen right away, but it would be several years before God would put my heart in His hands and cause it to beat again. Eventually, all of my pain and disappointment with God and myself came to the surface, and I was forced to face it. When I faced the pain, trauma, and disappointment, God was able to bring truth and perspective into my relationship with Him. He was not the one who had caused my pain, yet He had seen it all. He let me see His relentless pursuit of my heart through all of the things I had walked through, and this brought a deep healing in my relationship with Him beyond anything I could have ever imagined. Now my heart would beat for Him and Him alone. After my heart was restored completely to Him, the Holy Spirit allowed the pain I had pushed down in other relationships to surface, dealing with each thing as I was ready. He would allow this because He wanted my heart to be made completely whole.

Healing What I Believed about God as a Father

One area the Holy Spirit wanted to bring wholeness was in my relationship with God the Father. The first round of healing began when my husband and I were looking at buying a new house. We found one we both really loved that was everything we thought we wanted. During this time, I became very emotionally triggered, and I could not understand what was going on. I processed with the Holy Spirit as my counselor, and what came to the surface was the belief that *what was important to me, was not important to God.* I ended up calling a good friend, and she began to minister to me. I let the Father bring healing to the pain and disappointment in this area, and I asked Him to forgive me for believing this lie.

Before this experience, I could never picture myself with the Heavenly Father. Shortly after, I was able to see myself as a three-year-old little girl, twirling around in joy as He watched me with loving admiration. I felt truly seen and celebrated. This experience brought a whole new level of healing to my heart. I began to trust the Father, and I started to believe that what was important to me, was *also* important to Him. It was one thing to know this in my head, but now I began to experience this on an emotional level.

Through this, and several other events, the Holy Spirit showed me that I not only believed this lie about my heavenly Father, but I also believed it about my husband. After I repented from this lie and changed what I believed, so did what I was experiencing in my life. I trusted the Father and my husband to take care of my needs and the desires of my heart, *and they did.* Once again, I saw the importance of my core beliefs and my agreement with truth concerning the Father's heart toward me.

> *Be careful how you think; your life is shaped by your thoughts (Proverbs 4:23 GNT).*

Healing My Heart from Rejection

In every area of my life, I experienced more and more healing and freedom. And yet, I still felt the pain of rejection from wounds that ran deep. Many times I thought these areas were fully healed, but later I realized that what I experienced was only one layer of healing.

Deep wounds tend to have deep roots, and sometimes they have to be healed in stages.

My moment of greatest breakthrough began when something was said to me that triggered the pain in this area. Instead of running from it, I set my heart to seek God and process with the Holy Spirit. As I did, the Holy Spirit began to open a window into my heart. He brought me to a childhood memory when something happened that made me feel like someone else was always more important. In that moment, I realized this lie had become a core belief, and so, it had become a self-fulfilling prophecy that manifested over and over again throughout my life.

Realizing where this lie had come in was an important moment for me, but it didn't make the pain go away. For months the pain of rejection was right below the surface, to the point of tears many times, and it never left me. Finally, I got to the end of my rope, and I was desperate to be free from this torment once and for all. I brought my heart to the altar of the Lord in surrender every day, and as I processed with the Holy Spirit, little things began to come to the surface. While I was walking and praying one day, the Holy Spirit began to quote the scripture, "You will know the truth, and the truth will set you free" (John 8:32 CSB). In that moment, I knew if I knew the truth about myself, I would be free.

After this, the Holy Spirit began to show me how I always felt people were rejecting me, even when they weren't. It was like an "ah ha" moment for me. I saw how I had filtered what many people said or did through this filter of rejection. Whether it was true or not, it was what I believed. The Holy Spirit then gave me this scripture:

Yahweh responds, "But how could a loving mother forget her nursing child and not deeply love the one she bore? Even if a there is a mother who forgets her child, I could never, no never, forget you. Can't you see? I have carved your name on the palms of my hands! Your walls are always my concern" (Isaiah 49:15–16 TPT).

As I read this verse, I began to weep in God's presence. Jesus pulled back the veil and through revelation from heaven, He showed me that He had taken all rejection on the cross, and it was impossible for me to be rejected because I was accepted in Him. I had believed that I was rejected, but this was a lie from the pits of hell. Right then and there, I asked God to forgive me for believing this lie and for blaming others for my feelings of rejection. I lingered in God's presence and let this truth go deep into my heart.

As I always do when He is working something into my life, I camped out on His Word until it became a part of me. I knew His truth needed to become more real to me than the lie I had believed all of those years. What I had perceived as rejection had tormented and crippled me for much of my life. As I repented (changed how I believed and came into agreement with the truth) I was released from a prison in my soul where the enemy had held me captive for far too long.

Even though I was helpless in the hands of my hateful, strong enemy, you were good to deliver me (Psalms 18:17 TPT).

Choosing Life

My mom once told me that when she drove up our driveway during my high school years, she never knew if she would find me dead or alive. I often contemplated taking my life because of my eating disorder. I felt like such a burden to my family, and many times, I started to lose hope of ever experiencing freedom.

Although I could not bring myself to take my life, there was a huge part of me that felt like life was just too hard. I was in so much pain, and being in heaven with Jesus seemed like a much better option. I didn't understand how wrong this kind of thinking was until the Holy Spirit began to show me that to not choose life was to not choose God.

> I call heaven and earth as witnesses today against you, that I have set before you life and death, blessing and cursing; therefore choose life, that both you and your descendants may live; that you may love the Lord your God, that you may obey His voice, and that you may cling to Him, for **He is your life** and the length of your days (Deuteronomy 30:19–20 NKJV, emphasis added).

As God was beginning to deal with this area of my life, I heard these words in my spirit: "You need to suck the milk out of life." In that very moment, my heart understood all that Jesus meant by that phrase. I began to see that it was such a dishonor to God for me not to enjoy my life because He *was* my LIFE. When I rejected life, I rejected Him. I asked Jesus to forgive me for my wrong mindset when I saw how much it had grieved His heart.

After this, I started to look at life very differently. I began to drink in the pure pleasures of living. I saw how Jesus took pleasure when I enjoyed a delicious meal, a good book, or a great movie. Jesus loved to see me fully present and enjoying my family and friends. In His eyes, all of these precious moments were sanctified and Holy because they were part of my life and gifts from Him. I realized that life was to be lived and enjoyed, not spent waiting for the day I would go home to Jesus. Oh, how wrong I had been about so many things.

> *Thou shalt also suck the milk of the Gentiles, and shalt suck the breast of kings: and thou shalt know that I the Lord am thy Saviour and thy Redeemer, the mighty One of Jacob (Isaiah 60:16 KJV).*

There was a drastic change in me after this, but it did not mean I would never have to deal with my "Beam me up, Scotty"[1] mentality again. When things would get hard in life, this mindset would pop up. There were so many lies attached to this part of my heart, but the deepest one was that the world would be better off without me. Many times I defeated this lie, and I would think I was completely free. Then a bit of time would pass and there it would be again, staring me in the face.

One such time was several years ago. I was struggling with these thoughts again when one of my friends gave me a prophetic word about being like a butterfly. She said that butterflies, although small, can influence weather on the other side of the world simply by flapping their wings. When she told me this, she had no idea I was fighting to see how my life had value. After she gave me the word, God brought to mind how my influence had helped my daughter make an important decision that changed her life forever. One day after she made this decision, she had an incredible encounter with God in her car. When it was over and she began to drive again, butterflies surrounded her vehicle and flew at the same speed she was driving for miles. She had told me about her experience and how incredible it was. This word about butterflies was God's way of showing me that my life really *did* matter.

Years after the prophetic word about butterflies, I was faced with a health challenge and the possibility that something very serious was wrong with me. When this happened, I was struggling to see my value again and thought maybe my purpose on earth was finished. During this time, God met me in a significant way in the book of Philippians. The apostle Paul longed for heaven, but he told God he would stay if it was for a greater good. I identified with Paul's desire to be with the Lord, but I felt God speaking to me once again, showing me I still needed healing in this area of my life.

A few days later, I got home from an important doctor's appointment, and my good friend called to see how I was doing. Before we got off the phone, she prayed for me. She asked God to send His light and His daily bread to reveal to me whatever I needed for that day. While she was praying, I saw myself as a teenage girl, when I had wanted to take my life and purposely slit my wrist. I told her about my vision, and she immediately said, "That's it. When you cut your wrist as a teenager, you made a covenant with death." As we talked about this, I felt waves of sadness washing over me. The Holy Spirit then showed me where the root of this sadness had come in. We prayed over this, and I asked God to forgive me for cutting my wrist and wanting to take my life. After we prayed, I physically felt something lift off of me.

After healing the roots where these lies came in, the Lord led me back to the book of Philippians. This time the words were jumping off the pages, infusing me with hope and ministering to me about my future. I could feel God restoring the joy that had been lost in past seasons. Around the same time, I connected with one of my precious sisters in the Lord who happens to be an artist. After we talked that day, she felt inspired to paint. And do you know what she painted? A butterfly! And she wanted to send it to me. She had no idea butterflies were significant to me when she painted this picture. Her painting is now in my living room, and it reminds me every day that my life really does matter.

> *My true life is the Anointed One, and dying means gaining more of him. So here's my dilemma: Each day I live means bearing more fruit in my ministry; yet I fervently long to be liberated from this body and joined fully to Christ. That would suit me fine, but the greatest advantage to you would be that I remain alive (Philippians 1:21–24 TPT).*

Chapter 14

Restoring the Foundations of Many Generations

I believe with every fiber of my being that the body of Christ is desperate and hungry, now more than ever, for a gospel that transforms us from the inside out. We long to see cycles of dysfunction healed so that it changes how we interact in our marriages and families. Many believers have read their Bibles, memorized scripture, prayed, fasted, and gone through deliverance, and yet they still have not seen the changes they long for. So many don't know where to go or what to do at this point. We must encounter the Jesus we read about in Isaiah 61 and experience what He proclaimed about Himself:

The Spirit of the Lord God is upon me, Because the Lord has anointed and commissioned me To bring good news to the humble and afflicted; He has sent me to bind up [the wounds of] the brokenhearted, To proclaim release [from confinement and condemnation] to the [physical and spiritual] captives And freedom to prisoners, To proclaim the favorable year of the Lord,

And the day of vengeance and retribution of our God . . . To grant to those who mourn in Zion the following: . . . The oil of joy instead of mourning, The garment [expressive] of praise instead of a disheartened spirit. So they will be called the trees of right-eousness . . . The planting of the Lord, that He may be glorified. Then they will rebuild the ancient ruins, They will raise up and restore the former desolations; And they will renew the ruined cities, The desolations (deserted settlements) of many generations (Isaiah 61:1–4 AMP).

This kind of transformation is possible when we completely surrender to love Himself. Jesus wants us to not only acknowledge our pain, but also invite Him into it. He wants to confront the heart-break and disappointment so He can heal us at the level of our iden-tity. We have been taught by a religious system that if we look good, we are good. So we pretend everything is all right to save face, but behind closed doors our hearts are broken and our families are still riddled with hidden dysfunction.

Jesus said He came for those who needed a physician, so our churches must become hospitals rather than show places. Our family, whether spiritual or natural, must become a safe place to confront pain, acknowledge it, and be healed. We all carry pain—pain from others and pain we have caused as well. To face our pain takes courage. It's much easier to live in a place of denial and continue to numb. No matter who we are, there is a temptation to do this in one form or another. It seems harmless, and no one cares if someone numbs their pain and the cost is small. But when the cost becomes a life altering addiction, that is another story. When this is the case, it can only stay hidden for so long before everyone becomes aware of it. Even if our pain does not manifest as a life altering addiction, it can still rob us of being fully present and walking in our true identity.

Breaking the Cycle

They say pain travels through families until someone is willing to face it. If you look at Isaiah 61, you will see that Jesus came to heal the broken-hearted and set the captive free—in that order. Could it be possible that our captivity came because of a broken heart? When you don't get to the root and heal the broken heart, you will see the same sin pattern repeat from one generation to the next. Families begin to change when one person has their broken heart healed and says yes to the process of walking out of captivity. Years of generational cycles can be healed when God's unconditional love comes into the place of our greatest brokenness.

The healing that began in my own life through knowing I was God's beloved opened the door for healing to begin in my husband and children's lives. I wanted them all to experience not just being saved and having a nice life, but I wanted my family to be free—truly free. I knew this would only happen if they came to a place of knowing their identity as His beloved. This is the answer to years of generational pain and dysfunction, and this alone will heal the broken heart.

Restoration in My Own Family

Because I wanted my relationship with my kids to be made whole, I invited them to come to me with their pain. It has not been fun or easy, but I asked them to come to me with anything I had done that caused them pain. Doing this has given me a chance to face any of the guilt I carried over mistakes I made, even ones I was not aware of. There were times I couldn't remember the things my children confronted me with, but I knew that what mattered was how they perceived things. I needed to be willing to face the pain I had contributed to, not only from what I had done wrong, but also from what I *hadn't* done. It was important for me to validate their feelings and not be defensive. Just to have someone listen and say, "I'm so sorry," makes such a difference to our hearts. It helps us get unstuck and move on from the pain.

During the last years of high school and the first few years of college, my youngest daughter and I had a very strained relationship. After she went through some hard things in college, our relationship began to change. I was able to be there to listen and love because of the healing work God had done in me. I was finally able to give my daughter the love and compassion she needed rather than judgment. This was just the beginning of restoration in our relationship. It took many painful, but truthful sessions of talking over many years. I don't think this would have happened if I had not allowed Jesus to heal me. I had to come to the place of being willing to be vulnerable. This was only able to happen as I became secure in my identity. My daughter and I are now very close, and she is one of my best friends. Because of her, I have learned how to be a better mother and a better listener. She has taught me what it looks like to validate someone's pain properly and how to love unconditionally without judgment. Through this process, we have both grown and changed. What God has done in our relationship is such a treasure to me.

Healing the Child Within

The more I've walked myself and others through healing, the more I've come to see that inside of every adult, there is a small child who still needs to grow up. When we are born again, our spirit comes into oneness with God, but our soul can still be very childish and immature. Transformation takes time, and it is a process that we say yes to. Sometimes it feels like two steps forward and one step back. We may look like a mature believer on the outside until a place of pain is triggered. All of the sudden, the wounded child inside of us makes an appearance. When we act out of character from how we would normally respond, you can bet it was our triggered child.

> *When I was a child, I spoke about childish matters, for I saw things like a child and reasoned like a child. But the day came when I matured, and I set aside my childish ways (1 Corinthians 13:11 TPT).*

When we are willing to face our pain, it gives our heavenly Father a chance to meet us there. When the Father speaks to that wounded child inside of us, we are able to move past our pain and that part of us is connected to Him again. As the revelation of Jesus (the righteous branch) grows inside of us, we grow up and no longer operate as immature children. As we grow and are transformed, we are restored back to God's original intent and our true identity.

> *For God is satisfied to have all his fullness dwelling in Christ. And by the blood of his cross, everything in heaven and earth is brought back to himself—back to its original intent, restored to innocence again! (Colossians 1:19–20 TPT)*

When one person's heart is healed and transformed, it opens the door for all of our generational lines to begin the healing process. As individuals heal, families will begin to transform. As families are transformed, cities are changed. As cities are changed, countries are changed, and as countries are changed, nations are transformed. This is how we disciple nations. It begins with one person who is completely yielded—with one person who will say yes to the transformation process that comes as a result of union with Jesus.

Chapter 15

Our Great Hope

I f you are at the end of my story, I pray it has opened your eyes to the hope there is in Jesus, and the power He has to restore even the most broken life. What makes me love the Lord so much is that He came not for those who are well, but for those who needed a physician.

> *Jesus overheard their complaining and said, "Who goes to the doctor for a cure? Those who are well or those who are sick? I have not come to call the 'righteous,' but to call those who know they are sinners and bring them to repentance" (Luke 5:31–32 TPT).*

From the time I was young, I realized my great need for God. He has taken the worst parts of my life and redeemed them. This is the nature of God, and this is who He is. He loves a redemption story, and He has a way of turning tragedy into triumph. It's what He does best.

Story of the Rug Weaver

Recently I was listening to a preacher. At the end of his message, he told a story about a very famous rug weaver. This rug weaver was known all over the world for his ability to make the most beautiful rugs in existence. One day, the rug weaver's daughter asked if he would teach her to make rugs like him. He took her under his wing, and they started to make a rug together. As they worked, he instructed her.

When the rug was finished, it was the most beautiful one he had ever created. Later, someone came to interview him about it, and they commented on his daughter saying, "She must have the same gift that you have, at six years old, to be a part of making a rug like this." He said, "I don't know . . . every stitch she made was wrong . . . [but] I anticipated her mistakes, and I wove them into the rug."[1]

This story unhinged my heart when I heard it because this is the God I have come to know. He knows every wrong decision we will make, but He knows exactly how to redeem them all. He is a loving God, full of grace and mercy, who takes even our worst mistakes and makes them something beautiful. He alone is our great and wonderful redeemer.

> You came near when I called you, and you said, "Do not fear."
> You, Lord, took up my case; you redeemed my life (Lamentations
> 3:57–58 NIV).

My own life feels a lot like this story. He has taken all of my mistakes and all of my brokenness, and He has woven them all into a beautiful tapestry. The front of the tapestry is a work of art, but if you turn it over to look at the back, it looks like a tangled mess. The process has been messy, but the Father knew me before the foundation of the world. He knew everything I would go through before I went through it. He has been my Alpha and Omega, my beginning and my end. He's been there all along watching over my days, always pursuing me. He knew the exact time my heart would be ready to deal with the things that robbed me of my true identity.

One day I was in a worship service, and I had a vision of myself when I was about sixteen years old. The Lord spoke to my heart, and this is what He said: "Remember that messed up teenage girl? Well, I saw her completely whole when I looked at her back then, and I always knew she would be where you are now."

When God looks at us, He does not see us through a timeline, but He sees the finished product. He sees us totally restored and completely redeemed. I thought about what He said, and I was able to see it. It was so simple. Of course He could see me that way, because He is God. He sees the beginning and the end. He was not looking at me and thinking to Himself *Man, I can't wait until she gets her act together.* As humans, we dwell in time, but God is outside of time and how He sees everything is different. We get so impatient with the process, but to Him, it is already finished. The only part we play is to come into agreement with what He has already accomplished.

It amazes me to think about the fact that all of those years ago, God saw me where I am now. He took pleasure in me even when I was at my worst, and He always knew I would become His beloved bride. He knew that I would choose Him and never stop following Him. I have come to a place where my heart is set like flint, knowing He is trustworthy because He has proven Himself to me time and time again.

Here's what I've learned through it all: Don't give up; don't be impatient; be entwined as one with the Lord. Be brave and courageous, and never lose hope. Yes, keep on waiting—for he will never disappoint you! (Psalms 27:14 TPT)

If you are reading this and feel like I did, like a failure, don't. He calls you His beloved, and He loves you unconditionally. Transformation is a process. Learn to enjoy the journey and enjoy Him. Let Him love you into wholeness. I promise He will transform you if you let Him. It's what love does. Love transforms the broken soul when nothing else will. He is the love you have been looking for all of your life. So let go! Say yes and MARRY HIM. His love will conquer all.

Notes

Everyone's Looking for Their Great Love Story

1. Liz Wright, "Jesus and the Bride w/ Dr. Brian Simmons," Live Your Best Life, May 17, 2021, YouTube video, 27:04, https://www.youtube.com/watch?v=IKOvhr_NYG8

1. Where It all Started

1. Margaret Johnson, *18, No Time to Waste* (Grand Rapids, MI: Zondervan Publishing House, 1971).
2. Catherine Marshall, *Something More: In Search of a Deeper Faith* (New York: McGraw-Hill, 1974).

2. How I Came to the End of Myself

1. Ray Boltz, "The Anchor Holds," recorded October 3, 1994, track 8 on *Allegiance*, Word Records, compact disc.

3. His Redeeming Love

1. Francine Rivers, *Redeeming Love* (New York: Multnomah Books, 1997).

7. Coming Into His Rest

1. Larry Lea, *Could You Not Tarry One Hour?: Learning the Joy of Prayer* (Lake Mary, FL: Charisma Media, 1987).
2. C.S. Lewis, *The Problem of Pain* (New York: HarperCollins, HarperOne, 2001), 91.
3. Lesotho Englebert, "Bob Jones' 100 Year Vision," Swiftfire with Shamael Wolverton, September, 26, 2009, YouTube video, 4:59, https://www.youtube.com/

watch?v=ZUrfpHr0-LM.

8. Cultivating and Protecting Connection

1. *Stepmom*, DVD, directed by Chris Columbus (Culver City, CA: Sony Pictures Home Entertainment, 1999).

9. The Word and His Words

1. "G4487 - rhēma - Strong's Greek Lexicon (kjv)." Blue Letter Bible. Accessed 4 Feb, 2022. https://www.blueletterbible.org/lexicon/g4487/kjv/tr/0-1/

10. Becoming a Believing Believer

1. Sarah Young *Jesus Calling: Enjoying Peace in His Presence* (Nashville, TN: Thomas Nelson, 2016).

13. Heart Made Whole

1. James Doohan, *Beam Me up, Scotty: Star Trek's "Scotty"—in His Own Words* (New York: Pocket Books, 1996).

15. Our Great Hope

1. Damon Thompson, "Carolina Revival - 3/21/21," March 23, 2021, in Damon Thompson Ministries, produced by Damon Thompson, podcast, MP3 audio, 1:43:42, https://podcasts.apple.com/us/podcast/carolina-revival-3-21-21/id618115914?i=1000514100121

About the Author

If you enjoyed *Marry Me* and would like to hear more from Kay, connect and follower her on:

- INSTAGRAM: @flysouthmagnolia
- BLOG: https://theunencumberedlife.wordpress.com

Made in the USA
Columbia, SC
08 March 2022

57402347R00085